Praise

'An outstanding attitude and w
— **Karren Brady CBE**

'I think Liv Conlon is reason enough to be so hopeful about the future. A young business leader with both entrepreneurial savvy and a strong commitment to purpose and contribution to society; she's just the young leader the world needs. I've no doubt this book will impact all who read it.'
— **Jessica Huie MBE**, Author of *Purpose*

'Liv's book is the step-by-step guide that I wish I had when I was starting out.'
— **Marc Randolph**, Co-Founder of Netflix

'Liv is an inspiration to everyone, regardless of age. Her work ethic is impeccable and I am constantly impressed by her creativity. She is a real beacon of hope for anyone looking for the motivation to take their future into their own hands and launch a business. Not only is her journey incredible but she gives you the blueprint to blaze your own trail on the entrepreneurial voyage.'
— **Mike Handcock**, Chairman of The Circle of Excellence Group

STAGER BOSS

How I Launched a 7-Figure
Home-Staging
Business in
Under 2 Years
– and How
You Can Too!

LIV CONLON

Rethink

This book is dedicated to every single woman inside our #StagerBoss Tribe – to those who have been told to dim their light or that they are too much, and to those women who are now ready to truly claim their time to shine.

Contents

1

How I 'Ruined' My Life

'You're ruining your life.' These words will always ring in my mind when I think back to the young and not-so-impressionable Liv as I sat in my high-school's careers office.

Earlier that week, teachers had handed out a form to every pupil who was of school-leaving age. The form asked us what we wanted to do with our lives. Do sixteen-year-olds really know that? I would say most don't; however, I did. I even knew the exact industry that I wanted to go into. I also knew that I didn't ever want to work for anyone else.

As I stared at the paper, I saw four boxes staring back at me:

- ✓ Progress into sixth form
- ✓ Apply for university / college
- ✓ Full-time employment
- ✓ Not sure

There was no 'other' option and I realised for the first time, this would be the theme for the rest of my life – not finding a box that I would fit in. Of course, being the rule breaker I am, I added my own box on the page:

- ✓ Launch my own business

At first, I was met by silence. I heard nothing back, which shocked me initially. Just as I concluded it must be a ridiculous form the teachers got us to fill in so they could meet their quota, the response came. During a maths period, I was asked to visit the careers officer in the support room.

'I've definitely sparked some interest,' I thought. 'An A-grade student not applying to become a doctor or lawyer? How scandalous.'

I had never met the careers officer in my life, which doesn't make a lot of sense. Because that's exactly what you want to do – share your hopes and dreams with a stranger. As I entered the small white room, I glanced out of a window on to the school yard.

Above the window was a clock – an identical clock hung on the wall of every classroom, hallway and dining hall in the school. It looked exactly the same as the one I had been staring at for years, willing time to move faster.

I greeted the careers officer – a woman – in a friendly manner and sat down in the seat across from her. After the usual pleasantries, the patronising tone began. She explained that she was speaking with me as she feared for my wellbeing, which I assumed meant she feared for the school's exam result statistics.

'Is everything OK at home?' Then she got to her point. I was on track for five As in my chosen subjects and I had a squeaky clean record at school, apart from the occasional sending out of the classroom for asking, 'When will I ever use this in real life?' (I have still never used Pythagoras's theorem or needed to find the value of X.) She was dumbfounded as to why I had created a box about starting my own business.

I proceeded to tell her that I was going to be leaving school upon the completion of my exams, regardless of my grades, and that I would be launching my home-staging business.

She replied, 'I don't even know what home staging is.'

I gave her my explanation, sharing with her what the term means. This is how the conversation went:

Liv: 'I will be furnishing and staging properties for sale, giving them a show-home look.'

Teacher: 'So, interior design?'

Liv: 'Well, sort of, but not really.'

Teacher: 'And who would pay you for that? You don't even have a degree; you should really consider Glasgow School of Art.'

Liv: 'I've looked into that. I don't believe I'll need to study for four years to get clients.'

And then the statement that would change my life forever:

'Well, Olivia, I really don't know why you aren't considering university and I would be seriously concerned if you were to launch a business now. You have your whole life to do that – what if it doesn't work? This is such a crucial time for you. You are ruining your life.'

The words hurt, just a little. In that moment, I could have gone back to my form and ticked the relevant box, but I didn't. Instead, I felt a familiar feeling that I've experienced many times. That feeling when someone tells you that you can't do something. It made me even more determined to do it. My cheeks grew red with anger.

Who the hell is this woman to tell me I can't do this?

I said, 'Well, Miss, I'm sorry you feel that way, but I'm doing it anyway.'

Little did I know this exact moment would become the story I would share with the world. I have told it many times, returning to my primary school to inspire pupils there, speaking on the TEDx stage, in my first best-seller *Too Big For Your Boots* and when I'm on stage sharing it with my all-female audience at #StagerBoss. My message is simple:

'Never accept being told to hide your light.'

That was a fast forward, so how did I get there? Well, it all started at the very moment I was told I couldn't do it.

Guess what? I bloody did! From finding my very first entrepreneurial spark at thirteen years old, when I started importing fake nails from China (thank you, Google and Alibaba), I discovered the business that would shape my future and predetermine every single thing I've achieved to this date when I turned sixteen.

People say that entrepreneurs fail a minimum of six times before they find the idea that sticks, the light-bulb moment. For me, I struck gold on idea #2. I had spotted a gap in the market and I had the gumption to fill it. Like many business ideas, mine didn't come to me when I was lying in bed; my home-staging business was born out of frustration.

My mum, Ali (one of my biggest inspirations in life and now my business partner), had been self-employed for twelve years. By day, she trained sales people in customer service and disability awareness in the car industry; by night, she was investing in property with the vision to retire both herself and my dad as soon as possible.

Her first property, a £50,000 flat that she bought at auction, would become my muse. The property already had a converted attic, but no planning permission for this conversion. Securing said planning permission with a new staircase installed was an instant way to increase the value, as it could then be marketed as a proper room. It was a two-bedroom property with an open-plan living, dining and kitchen area. However, the untrained eye – which is the majority of the population – couldn't see this vision.

The feedback from those who viewed the property was that it was 'really' a one-bedroom apartment. They couldn't see that the *huge* kitchen begged to be an open-plan living area so the other reception room could be used as a second bedroom.

The property was empty when it was listed on the market and it wasn't selling or even generating much interest. Three months had passed and something had to be done. Unsurprisingly, the estate agent suggested that we lower the price (they like to do that) but it wasn't an option for us. We had to achieve the highest sale price possible.

An empty property tends to look smaller than a furnished space as there is no furniture as a frame of reference. And so, I suggested staging it.

Having been dragged around home-decor shops as a child, seen home-renovation shows and been taken along to one of the property investment courses that my mum had attended, I was aware of staging. I soon realised, however, the rest of the UK hadn't heard of it. . . yet. When I looked for a company with the potential to stage the property for us, the Google search didn't produce any decent companies to provide the service – certainly not any with prices that weren't astronomical. And so, I realised, if we wanted this staged, we would have to do it ourselves.

I asked my mum for her budget, and then I staged the property. I presented the open-plan living-kitchen space as it should be used. The results spoke for themselves when the property went back on the market, staged, and quickly silenced the 'price-dropping' agent:

- **Before staging:** on the market for three months.

- **After staging:** on the market **for three days.**

- **Before staging:** no offers.

- **After staging:** an offer £5k above the valuation and an extra bonus ££: the client purchased all of the furniture.

It was still the same property.

It was still the same four walls.

It was still with the same agent.

My first experiment with staging proved that it works. ('Staging works': someone should put that on a T-shirt. Oh wait, I already have.) It proved to me that if staging could work for my mum's property, then it could work for others, and I knew that if I could share my success story with the world, there would be a demand for this service.

The only issue was, I was sixteen years old. I had no start-up funds to get this idea off the ground. I didn't have a design degree or any design qualifications for that matter; I didn't have a portfolio; I didn't even have any life experience.

How was I going to make this work?

My First Client

Fast forward to me leaving school. Still only sixteen, I took my tender age, long curly blonde hair and baby face into what was a male-dominated industry. Walking into networking events full of middle-aged men was daunting, never mind trying to convince them that cushions and artwork would help sell or rent their properties faster. I even cut my long curly blonde hair into a pixie style in a bid to look five years older, but to begin with, I struggled to secure that elusive first client.

However, I did manage to secure a thirty-minute speaking slot at a local property networking event. I had never presented in front of anyone before, apart from my school peers, and when I think back now, my presentation at that networking event wasn't very good. But when you're so bad at something, the only way is up.

I couldn't have been that bad, though, or maybe it was that Paula had a soft spot for me. Either way, she approached me after my presentation and asked me to stage her two-bedroom property in Glasgow, Scotland.

I had my first client, Paula.

#StagerBoss trivia: we have an annual awards ceremony at #StagerBoss, and the first award students can win is the 'I Got My Paula'. This is for every student who secures their first client. The client may be called Bob or Jane, but the award is called Paula. . . after my first client :)

You'll learn more about #StagerBoss in the next chapter. For now, let's get back to my first client.

Paula's property was on one of the roughest streets in Glasgow in a location where the average life expectancy is only sixty-three. It was being marketed for £60,000. I was ecstatic: someone had trusted me to stage their property, but how would I do it?

After working out what I could buy, I budgeted for the cheapest sofa I could source. I planned to pick up a bed from Gumtree (the UK's Craigslist) and 'borrow' some bedroom lamps from my family home, using a blanket as a living-room rug (with a whopping cost of £5). I worked out I could stage the property for £1,897 and would charge Paula £2,000.

I didn't have the cash. But I knew I could do it. I just had to find a way to make it work.

Then the idea came to me: I would ask Paula for the payment upfront.

Paula was a little hesitant at first to transfer £2,000 to a sixteen-year-old, but she did so. I purchased the goods and staged the property, making a dazzling £103 profit on my first installation.

You may be thinking, 'How is this going to be life-changing, Liv?' Here's the gold.

Paula was only renting the furniture from me for six weeks. Meaning that after those six weeks were up (when I'd estimated the property would be sold, and it was), I would be on the hunt for my next client. However, when I staged the next property, I would already own the kit of furniture.

This meant that if I charged the same again, all I would now have to pay for was the removal of the kit from the first property to the second property. On the assumption that my removal costs would be 10% of what I charged, I would now be in profit of £1,800.

And I could rent that kit again and again and again.

The switch had flipped. This was it. This was the business I would go *all in* on. Little did I know this would be *the* business model that would not only go on to support me in creating a seven-figure home-staging business in under two years, but also help thousands of women create their own wealth via this exact business model.

Knowing I was on to something, I used the exact same model time and time again. I built my business staging properties from one single kit, moved around in my ten-year-old Vauxhall Corsa once I had passed my driving test. (That car, unfortunately, was condemned when it was accidentally hit by a forklift at my 100sqft warehouse.) I now own over forty kits, stage more than 400 properties each year, service other property sectors and, with my amazing team, generate seven-plus figures in annual revenue.

I achieved all this before I was even out of my teens. Don´t let age be a barrier!

2

Welcome To The Rest Of Your Life

OK, now you know the story of how I launched my seven-figure home-staging company, let's get down to business. This book may not be what you're expecting; in fact, it's probably going to be better.

Bear with me. Yes, this is a book about building a home-staging business and it will act as your start-up guide, giving you the exact steps for how to launch your own home-staging business. I'll be sharing the exact strategies and map I used to launch my business from ZERO and scale it to a seven-figure success in under two years while still in my teens.

But it's not the strategies or the practical advice that I share within these pages that will change your life; it'll be a moment where something will awaken in you and it will be different for every reader. You'll know it; you won't be able to ignore it; it'll be a calling. You won't be able to sleep at night because you won't be able to stop thinking about launching this business. You'll look at your current life differently and accept that you want more.

That is my goal with this book. To awaken you to what is possible and reassure you that, no matter where you are or what you've been through, you can do this. I know because I've done it.

I'll be sharing the parts of my story that I want to hide, but I know that in doing so, I have the potential to impact your life forever. So, you've been warned: your life is about to change. This is your last chance to turn back. . .

You're still here? Great!

Are you feeling a hint of scepticism or questioning why I'm sharing all of my secrets with you? Are you wondering why I'm coaching women to open up in competition with me? Am I not worried they'll 'steal' my business, my clients, or copy me? Don't worry; I would wonder, too.

While it is my intention to support and coach women to establish their own brand in the market, of course this thought has popped into my mind. Although I'm a fairly prominent player in the United Kingdom,

I don't own the market. But here's the thing: I'm doing it anyway for these three reasons:

1. **I believe in collaboration over competition.** The home-staging industry is in its infancy, meaning we have a lot of work to do together as a community to spread the word and make staging an industry standard when it comes to selling a property. Together, we can grow this industry faster than going it alone.

2. **There is enough room for everyone.** I genuinely believe there is enough business out there for everyone. If we believed there was only space for one company in an industry, we would live in a boring world with one supermarket, one clothing store and one car brand. There need to be multiple businesses to serve the market at each level and cater for different budgets.
   Also, people buy from people and the reason someone will buy from you is totally different to why they'll buy from me. I'll teach you how to identify your brand story and uniqueness throughout this book.

3. **This is my calling.** It might shock you to know that building my home-staging business is not my calling. My true calling is to empower women to create financial independence using entrepreneurship as the tool. . . this is my addiction and it will become evident in the coming chapters why this is.

Don't get me wrong; my home-staging business, ThePropertyStagers, is still my core and most successful enterprise and I *love* what the team and I create. I still run the company to this day with my incredible mum. Integrity is one of my core values, therefore it's important to me that you know I love home staging and I'm still very much in the game. But I have also designed my life in a way that I get to fulfil my calling through serving you via #StagerBoss.

So, here is my promise to you over the next few hundred pages that we will share together. Everything I teach is proven and implemented in my own business. I don't teach anything that I have not personally used and I don't teach strategies that worked ten years ago; I am still implementing everything that I teach to this day.

I believe it's important that I highlight this as the home-staging industry is not regulated – there are no recognised accreditations, certifications or associations. It's crucial to me that my integrity is upheld and what I teach delivers results, period!

When I work with a mentor or an expert, I require that what they teach, they practise. They have to be where I want to go. I only take advice from experts who have achieved what I would like to achieve, are currently active and own an operating business in their industry. This is the *only* way they can hand me the map on how to get there too.

I'll be 100% transparent. There is no point in me sugar-coating what it's like to build a home-staging business. That would be doing you a disservice. Why? Well, if I were to sugar-coat the facts, when you go to launch and run your business, you'd have no idea what to expect and likely give up when the going gets tough. I personally like to know what is ahead of me.

Now, of course, everyone's journey is personal and I can't predict your exact circumstances. However, in sharing my full journey, the good, the bad and the ugly, I will give you an honest picture. You can learn from my mistakes, which will fast track your success and save you a lot of time and heartache.

As I say to my #StagerBoss students, 'Everything I teach you has a purpose. I don't teach it for the fun of it; everything is from my own experience.' Whether you take the advice or not is down to you, but I can assure you, following my advice will bring you success, fast.

This is why I created #StagerBoss. I want to help fast track your success and condense a decade into just a few short months for you.

The Story Of #StagerBoss

So, full disclosure (as I promised). When I initially launched #StagerBoss, I had no plans to build a brand or write a book, but I was asked constantly, 'How do you do it?' And frankly, I didn't have enough time to reply, advise and coach every person who DMed me via socials, so as a way to serve some of my audience, I decided to launch a one-day event: 'Supercharge Your Home-Staging Business'.

Ten people joined me in London for a full day and I imparted all of my knowledge to them, teaching them the exact roadmap of how to build a seven-figure home-staging business. There were over 800 slides that I had downloaded my brain on to; my attendees must have left brain-fried. If you've been to one of my #StagerBoss events, you'll likely know the feeling I'm referring to. Funnily, the launch event for this book was hosted in the exact same five-star hotel in the very same room with ten times the people attending.

After the success of the one-day event, the people spoke and I realised *one* day in *one* location wasn't enough. Some attendees couldn't make it or weren't based in the UK, so I turned that one-day event into my signature online course 'Staging Business Secrets'. Now anyone anywhere in the world could benefit from it.

Fast forward a few years and my team and I have trained tens of thousands of women globally online.

We have created and launched many new initiatives, from online programmes to our annual #StagerBoss LIVE conference, our mastermind programme, intimate retreats that I host at my home in Spain and our most prestigious programme with our high-level inner-circle members. We host a top-rated podcast and now I have published #*StagerBoss* the book.

But what is more incredible than all of this combined are the women we've attracted into our #StagerBoss Tribe – women from all over the world, different backgrounds and different walks of lives. We are a community of empowered women, unapologetically following our dreams and making them happen. If you've been to one of our events or joined us online, I'm sure you feel this power.

Our mission? To empower 1 million women globally to create financial independence via building their home-staging business. If you are not already a part of it, we can't wait to welcome you to the tribe.

The #StagerBoss Launch Method

Over the next eleven chapters, I'm going to walk you through what it takes to build a home-staging business from zero without any start-up funds, experience, portfolio or prior connections in the industry. It's possible; I'm not the only person to have done it. Thousands of the women who have been part of the #StagerBoss programmes have done it too. The #StagerBoss Launch Method I will describe in this book is intended to be used as your guide.

In each chapter, I will explain the strategy and share practical advice on how to implement all the methods. There is even an action list at the end of each chapter of everything you need to do. The reason behind my success is that I take consistent daily action, so to ensure you don't just read this book and throw it on to a shelf, never to look at it again, you'll find a full list of all the action points from all of the chapters at the end. Upon completion of the book, you'll know that you've carried out all of the first steps to launch your home-staging business.

In the next chapter, we'll look at why you're here. I like to look at your *why* in a different way. I believe there are two different fuel sources we can tap into to drive us forward: pain or purpose. For the first time ever, I'm going to share with you the real driver behind my success and how I've been able to channel my pain into creating a successful business, transitioning that pain into a higher power. Expect to have a revelation and a moment of clarity on what drives you right now and what will drive you moving forward.

In the fourth chapter, we will look at gaining clarity on the life you want to create, so that the chapters that follow will ensure you are designing and building a business that is aligned with the vision you have.

Not only are you going to get creative by mapping out your vision on your vision board, but I am going to help you identify your short- and long-term goals, ensuring that they are realistic and achievable. Let's get ready to dream!

In Chapter 5, perhaps one of the most exciting chapters, I'm going to be sharing with you the incredible business model that I've created to scale a seven-figure business with *zero* start-up funds. My goal with this chapter is that you will walk away knowing exactly how many properties you need to stage per year in order to replace your nine-to-five income with your dream income. You'll see how you can easily replace your income, working a whole lot less while doing something you love. This is going to blow your mind!

In Chapter 6, I'm going to walk you through the different services you can offer in your home-staging business (there are many opportunities for multiple streams of income). It may seem obvious, but most of these services are not well known and #StagerBoss is the only home-staging training company that teaches two of the services that are most lucrative to your business. These two services help make up our seven-figure per year revenue.

Would you like to attract a £250k client? Well, in Chapter 7, I'm going to share with you how I've found multiple six-figure dream clients and how you can too. I'll share with you how to identify who your dream client is, build out a client avatar and, most importantly, how to attract these game-changing clients by understanding them like no one else does.

Branding has been a game changer for me and my business. When you are in the home-interior game, your brand is an extension of your staging. In Chapter 8, I'm going to share with you how I built a household brand in under two years (even after a pivotal rebrand). I'll help you choose a brand name, look and feel, as well as extending beyond that to really mastermind how you want people to feel and think about your brand name when it pops up.

Do you want to build your business fast? Well, of course you do! In Chapter 9, we'll talk about the strategy that I attribute my success to: all things personal branding. Think of this like pouring accelerant on to the growth of your business. We'll be looking at identifying why people will buy from you and how to communicate your unique brilliance via your brand pillars.

Get ready to launch! I have promised you that this book will be your home-staging business launch guide, so of course, we've got to talk about making a splash on the scene with your new brand and service in Chapter 10. I'll be sharing the biggest mistakes I've made when it comes to launching, but also how

I've successfully launched three brands and attracted lots of attention with no ad spend.

I found my first client (my Paula) while out networking and speaking at an event where my dream clients were congregated. In Chapter 11, we're going to look at the best methods to find your first clients offline: think networking events and building relationships with key contacts. Selling one-to-one will help you build the confidence before exploding your brand online and selling one-to-many.

Get ready to go out to the masses and spread your marketing message far and wide by sharing your brand online. In Chapter 12, I'm going to show you how to set up your business on social media, design content that cuts through the noise and speak directly to those you want to work with, cementing your reputation both locally and nationally. Of my clients, 80% come from my online marketing methods and I'm going to share the exact strategies I use.

In Chapter 13, I'm going to bring you full circle and share with you some of the success principles that I've embodied over the last decade to create an industry-recognised brand and achieve all of the personal goals I've set. Remember, I have collected all of the chapter action lists together at the end of the book to serve as your go-to overall launch-guide action list.

Scorecard

Do you think you have what it takes to become a #StagerBoss? If so, I've designed a scorecard for you to complete at www.StagerBossTheBook.com/scorecard.

This is a set of questions designed to score you on the areas in which you need to excel to build a successful home-staging business, resulting in a customised report based on your answers. The results of the scorecard will give you a starting point, showing you the areas that you are currently strong in and those you need to focus on.

Ready? Let's do it!

3

Choose Your Fuel Source

There is a reason you have a copy of this book in your hands; it's not a coincidence. You want more than where you're currently at.

It can be hard to admit and it's even harder for others to accept. But you've come to the right place; I've got you. Perhaps you hate your nine to five and you're hungry to do something you love and feel like your skills and talents are truly appreciated. You're ready to do something for yourself, put your own oxygen mask on first. It may even feel like a relief to read those words; you can do this for *you*. Or perhaps home staging has always been your dream career.

If you want more, which I believe you do, you're in the right place at the right time. Right about now, you'll be getting a certain feeling while reading this. For me, I can feel it manifests in the pit of my stomach. It's like a fire, a burning desire. It can bring up a whole range of emotions, including excitement and/or fear.

Launching a business isn't easy; you have chosen a difficult path. Unless you've launched a business previously, you're entering into the unknown. Your mind is going to try to stop you from making this decision, because as humans, we're designed to avoid danger and launching a business is scary. The fear you feel is a primitive human response, so your mind will come up with many reasons why you shouldn't do it.

Have no fear, though; I have a strategy to combat that. I learned this strategy from personal development guru Mel Robbins: it's called the 5 Second Rule.[1] We all have five seconds to make a decision before our subconscious gets to work and tells us why we shouldn't do it, so we simply count to five, and make the decision.

I like to relate this to jumping into a pool. If I run and jump in immediately, I do it. If I stand at the edge of the pool and look into the water, my mind will start to think of all the reasons I shouldn't go in. It'll be cold; I'll get wet and have to wash my hair. And it's similar with launching your business. If you overthink it,

---

1   Robbins, M *The 5 Second Rule: Transform your life, work, and confidence with everyday courage* (Post Hill Press, 2017)

you won't take that leap of faith. It may mean leaving behind a career you've been in for a long time that gives you job security. It may mean going after the dream even though your family and friends think you are crazy.

I want you to promise me that throughout our time together, you will not *overthink* and you will take *action*. You will count to five and go *all in*.

Ready?

So, welcome! Welcome to living outside your comfort zone. The good news? The reason you're feeling this way, the reason you want more, is the very reason that is going to help you make it.

Now, don't close this book or skip ahead. I know it's tempting to want to learn the how immediately, but in thinking you're getting ahead, you'll be holding yourself back. I remember the exact same feeling as I sat in a $12million mansion in LA, having just invested in a $25,000 mastermind to take my business to the next level. I was hungry for the how. I wanted all of the strategies and I wanted to implement them all yesterday.

Can you imagine how I felt when my coach said, 'For the next four days, we'll be working on you and not the business'? I wanted to leave.

But the secret of how to achieve massive success is in this chapter.

If you were to ask me how I achieved what I did, I could give a plethora of clichéd answers such as 'work hard' or 'never give up'. And yes, while I actually stand behind both of these strategies, there has been a deeper driving force at the root of why I've worked so hard, why I've never given up. Being able to tap into that fuel source is why I'm where I am today. And if you learn in this chapter how to tap into your fuel source, you'll be, as Sia sang, *Unstoppable*.

I left you in Chapter 1 with an incomplete narrative. I shared my origin story of how I came up with the idea for ThePropertyStagers, but not how I built it to what it is today. Inside each of the chapters from now on, I am going to share with you a new part of my story, a piece of the strategy that I applied to grow the business. Literally anyone in the world could pick up this book, implement the teachings and build a wildly successful home-staging company, but few will. Why? Because they'll give up when it gets hard, and trust me, it gets *very* hard. The question is, what is it that keeps you going in those moments you want to give up?

The answer: your why, aka your fuel source.

Think of your car. It wouldn't move without fuel to propel it forward. We are exactly the same: we need something to fuel us / propel us towards our goals.

Don't confuse your fuel with your vision. Your vision is what will motivate you and pull you forward; I always think of my vision as my reward for the work I do. We will look at your vision in the next chapter. Your why, your fuel source, pushes you up the metaphorical hill. It's your fire. Think of it like this: if you're being both pushed and pulled up a mountain, you're going to get to the top a whole lot quicker than if you're only being pulled.

In my experience, there are two different fuel sources you can tap into. There is no right or wrong; it depends on the personal 'season' you are in. However, one fuel source has a time limit on how long you can tap into it for.

Your Short-Term Fuel Source: Pain

Having interviewed hundreds of successful entrepreneurs via my podcast, my biggest quest was to work out the one thing that most of them had in common. I discovered that in the initial few years of building their businesses, they were fuelled by pain. This looked different for every person: a past trauma; a loss of someone they loved; being rejected or fired. For some, it was the real and immediate pain that if they didn't make their business a success, they'd be broke or homeless. For me, this was an eye opening but also comforting discovery, because my success too has been fuelled by pain.

The first time that I tapped into pain as a fuel source was at high school. A group of girls bullied me, maliciously targeting me, making my life hell and pushing me to leave school early. They made me seek out ways to escape, but instead of channelling my pain into unproductive channels such as drink or drugs, I thankfully channelled my pain into launching my business. I dreamed of the day I would be incredibly successful, fantasising that one day they would be looking at me and regretting how horrible they'd been. Spoiler alert: that day came.

I now feel grateful for this pain (at the time, not so much). Without it, I may not have left school and started on my journey.

I realise for me, I flipped what was a painful experience into a positive experience; I appreciate that others aren't so lucky in turning things around. The secret is in the awareness to look at your current situation and ask, 'How can I use this to fuel me?'

It was a lightbulb moment for me when I realised that my pain was one of the most invaluable fuel sources I possessed, but little did I know then that I would continue to tap into it. It wasn't only school bullies and a pessimistic teacher who were drivers behind my success; there was another reason I got out of bed every day and went to work eighteen hours, seven days a week for two years. Yes, it was pain, but it was also necessity.

This part of my journey has taken me years to share. I tried to write a chapter on the pain I felt in my first book and I couldn't bring myself to publish it. The first time I shared this publicly, I was hosting the first #StagerBoss LIVE conference in London and I knew it was time. I knew that the women sitting in the room would have been through something similar, knew that in sharing my story, I would enable them to draw inspiration from it. The second time I shared it publicly was in my TEDx talk.[2] And the third time. . . in these pages.

Why didn't I share it sooner? Because I wasn't ready and that is OK.

I grew up in a sheltered middle-class family with two incredibly hard-working parents who were inspirational and encouraged me to go after my dreams. When I launched my business at the age of sixteen, I had been pushed by my doubters and pulled by my vision. But the excitement of launching my new business quickly disappeared as my life was turned upside down.

Without warning, my dad left.

My world came crashing down. I questioned every value that had been instilled in me and rapidly headed towards a dangerous path of self-destruction. I had

---

2   L Conlon (no date), 'The immeasurable power of sharing your story', TEDx Talks, www.youtube.com/watch?v=WZDrk1VythU

launched a business hoping for the financial and emotional support of both parents, and what happened was I witnessed my mum being left distraught with a heap of debt after working so hard her whole life. And so I had two options: give up and let life happen to me (which is what I felt like doing) or do something about it. Thankfully, I chose option two.

Again, I used pain as fuel to drive me. While it wasn't my responsibility to pay off that debt, my mum and I are a team and I knew we had to get out of this position together. I asked her to join me in my mission and together we built the business.

Why did I work as hard as I did? I didn't have a choice and I believe this is the true power of tapping into pain as your fuel source. When something is a *should* – 'I *should* get clients and build the business' – it's hard to possess the willpower and discipline to carry it out. When it is a *must* – 'I *must* build this business to keep a roof over my head' – you tap into a strength, discipline and work ethic you may not even have been aware that you had at your disposal.

And so we did what we had to do, my mum and me. We worked long hours. There was a whole lot of laughing; there was also a whole lot of tears, self-doubt and the daily questioning if we were doing the right thing in building this business together. We used every penny we earned to pay down the debt we owed and create a seven-figure business. As best-selling author

Jon Gordon said, 'Failure is not meant to be final and fatal. . . It is meant to refine you to be all that you are meant to be.'[3]

In sharing the driving force behind my success, I don't want you to feel sorry for me. I am not a victim. There are many people in the world who have suffered so much more than I have. I share this because I want you to know that no matter where you are right now, no matter what hardship or trauma you are going through, you can do this. You too can use your pain as your short-term fuel source.

Ask yourself:

- Is pain driving you currently?
- Can you use this as a fuel source to drive you to your vision?

Pain delivered results for me. I'm pretty certain it will deliver results for you too. It's been a way to unlock my potential and achieve massive success. However, along the way, I realised that using pain had become an addiction for me *because* it delivered results.

While there are no right or wrong fuel sources, I believe that pain needs to be a short-term option. Although this can drive you to create an extraordinary business,

---

3   Gordon, J (@JonGordon11) 'Failure is not meant to be final. . .' [tweet] 30 November 2015, https://twitter.com/JonGordon11/status/1459881688499200005, accessed 28 December 2022

at some point, your pain tank will be empty. Thankfully, there is another more empowering fuel source you can use. I'm no master, but I'm learning to tap into the fuel source called *purpose*.

Purpose As Your Fuel Source

While most successful entrepreneurs have used their pain to build successful businesses, the key is that they have only used it in the short term. They now succeed with purpose fuelling them.

OK, confession time. For years, I've watched successful actors, singers, entrepreneurs and presenters who have experienced the height of their careers and have more money in the world than most of us would know what to do with and I've found myself asking, 'Why do they keep working?' I thought I couldn't be bothered if I were them.

It's funny because I've found myself in a similar position. I don't mean that I'm in an untouchable financial position or that I've reached the height of my career, not at all, but for so long, my big goal was to pay off debt. It was the reason why I got out of bed in the morning and worked so hard. Frankly, there was no choice. And for so long, somewhat strangely, I dreaded the day I wouldn't have this debt anymore. I became addicted to the struggle.

And so the day that I transferred the final cash and paid off the last penny of debt, there was a sense of achievement and relief, but there was also a moment of panic. If I didn't have this driving me, how would I continue to motivate myself? As a result, I embarked on a journey of finding my purpose. I looked to these successful figures I had been watching and I modelled their methods.

To tap into the fuel source of purpose, there are several different elements you need. First comes serving others. I have now been in business just short of a decade and it is no surprise to me that good business is based on serving others. I've successfully built my business model on this, but not to the level I truly need to. My model was based on me escaping my pain, service being a by-product of that. As Robin Sharma says, 'He who serves the most, reaps the most, emotionally, physically, mentally and spiritually. This is the way to inner peace and outer fulfilment.'[4]

I've committed to purpose over profit and a deep dedication to really impacting lives. I do this through serving my home-staging clients at a deeper level than just staging their properties; rather, I get to know them and learn how I can ease their stress and pain. This ultimately led to me launching #StagerBoss, where I can deeply impact and change women's lives. The feeling of hosting my mastermind clients at my

---

4   Sharma, RS *The Monk Who Sold His Ferrari: A fable about fulfilling your dreams and reaching your destiny* (Harper Thorsons, 2015)

home where we sit around the dinner table and they share how their lives have been impacted by this experience is so humbling. My coaching clients, some of whom have become unrecognisable from who they were when I first met them, are worth more than any sale or amount of money.

The next element is charity. I've launched my charity (which had been a goal of mine for years), Too Big For Your Boots. It works with young people up to the age of twenty-one from low-income backgrounds to help them launch businesses and we do this through placing our training courses into schools. I personally mentor ten young people on their start-ups.

The third element is people. In building my business, I feel the weight of responsibility in how I impact my team, along with the clients, contractors and suppliers that we work with.

At times, entrepreneurship can feel like a selfish endeavour. Yes, you are allowed to build your business to satisfy your own purpose, but ultimately, it is one of the most selfless journeys, given that you impact your family, your internal and external teams (and their families), your clients (and everyone in their lives) and anyone who consumes your content and brand. No matter what personal season you are in and what fuel source is currently driving you, know that there is no judgement. All I ask is that you have awareness of whatever is the driving force behind your success. It is an unbelievably powerful tool to help you in building a dynamic and successful home-staging business.

Chapter Action List

Knowledge without action won't take you to success; action is always key. The action you need to take for this chapter is to answer these three questions:

- Is pain driving you currently?

- Can you use this as a fuel source to drive you to your vision?

- How can you tap into purpose as a fuel source?

4

Design Your Vision And Map Out Your Goals

'I need to create a new vision board.' As I drew a big green tick next to the elusive TEDx talk on my vision board, I found myself feeling slightly uneasy as I asked myself, 'What is next?'

Over the past few years, I'd been able to achieve every single item on that board. I don't share that with you to show off or brag in any way, but to show what is possible when you visualise, feel and put what you want out to the universe.

Because here's the thing: I can pinpoint how I made a lot of things happen on my board, eg, the dream house or the dream car. I worked hard, invested in myself and took big risks in order to achieve many of my goals financially, but the way I manifested them, I accredit to my vision.

The exact vision that I had for my dream home appeared on the estate agent's website at the exact time I was looking. The Range Rover I bought myself for my twenty-first birthday was looking impossible: it was out of stock and I struggled to find insurance anywhere because of my age, but somehow everything aligned and I signed for the car on 26 August (my birthday). I had built a prolific personal brand and a TEDx talk was on my vision board, but this privilege is by application only and I had to audition to speak. Lo and behold, a message from TEDx dropped into my direct messages (DMs) on Instagram, inviting me to do a talk (which is now available on YouTube, go check it out). Don't tell me that it was just coincidence; this all happened through the power of attraction and getting clear on what I wanted to create. . . oh, and lots of action.

It all started with a vision, which is why I want to deep-dive into this with you today. When you're creating your vision, I want you to dream *big*. Don't ask how you will achieve it – that will only limit you to restrictive thinking.

After you've visualised the business and life you want to create, we'll map out your goals. The two things can often be confused as being the same thing, but they're not. Your vision – the attractive and compelling new life – is what will pull you; the goals are what will hold you accountable and measure your success along the way. Think of it like stepping stones to how you'll achieve your vision.

My Method For Designing A Compelling Vision

Don't underestimate it. Whenever I need to sit down and reassess my vision, I often find myself putting it off or delaying it. I feel like it's an indulgent task, to sit, dream and start pinning visuals on to my Pinterest board, while my never-ending to-do list continues to grow. However, if I think about it logically, I would never get into a car without a destination in mind, so why would I aimlessly take action in my business when I don't know the destination I'd like to end up at?

If you're feeling this way, a mindset shift is required. There is no better way to spend your time than to consider in which direction you are heading. Some of my biggest game-changing decisions have come from these moments of quiet dreaming. And this is confirmed by my favourite quote of all time from author and copywriter Gary Halbert:

'Properly exploited, one good idea that occurs to you while walking on a beach is more than ten lifetimes of hard work.'[5]

Change your environment. Creating a compelling vision is not a task to do at the same desk that you work at every day or surrounded by the same four walls you live in. This is going to limit your creativity. How can you think beyond where you are now if you're still there?

Whenever I'm scheduling a day to reset or realign my vision, I seek an environment that inspires me. This is often a five-star hotel (occasionally including an overnight, where I truly escape and sit in the silence), or it may be sitting outside at the beach. The sea just oozes expansion. Purposely take time in an inspirational environment with no distraction at all.

Don't judge. When you're creating your vision, there is no asking 'How?', only dreaming. You want to create a realistic representation of what you want your life to look like.

If there were an award for my biggest critic, I would win. What I mean by that in this context is, I've found myself in the past putting on my vision board what I think I should have on there, when in fact, it's not

---

5   Halbert, GC 'Big Idea:' The Gary Halbert letter www.
     thegaryhalbertletter.com/newsletters/zhzz-07_big_idea.htm,
     accessed 22 November 2019

my dream. No matter how boring your vision may appear or how unrealistic it may feel at the moment, having no judgement is key.

Start with categories and let them flow. Nothing is off limits when it comes to creating your vision board. I like to get my creative juices flowing by thinking first and foremost about what I want my life to look like rather than my business. Why? Because I want to build an amazing life that is supported and financed by my business, not the other way around.

Here are some prompts to help you build out your vision board:

My life

- My dream home and car
- My family and relationships
- My perfect day (describe in detail what this looks like and how you'll feel)
- My dream vacation and trips
- Traditions that I want to create
- My health and fitness
- How I feel
- How I'm giving back financially and with my time

My business

- My perfect working day

- My team

- My office

- My role

- My clients and how I'm impacting them

- My launches or events

- My business achievements: awards, features, speeches, etc

- How my business integrates with my lifestyle

Add timelines and milestones. Giving yourself a deadline for when you want to achieve something will add a layer of added pressure to make it happen. However, with my vision, I like to apply these deadlines loosely. For example, I add an age I'd like to have achieved something by. My goals are where I get more dialled in on specific timings.

Be specific. If you tell the world you want more money, it can present you with a dollar on the ground and you're richer than you were ten minutes ago. Be as specific as possible when designing your vision. Find an image or describe in detail the exact dream kitchen you want, the specific financial goal and the precise feelings you want to feel when you achieve that goal.

Understand what method works for you. When you come to brainstorm your vision, there are a handful of ways to document this. For me, I am a visual person and seeing my vision every day is very powerful in reminding me of the bigger picture. I like to start with a large piece of blank card and pin on to it images of what I want my life to look like. I also like to open a blank document on my computer and type out words that empower me or explain what I want to create. I print these off and, just like in school, I use my glue stick to fix them to the big piece of card. Once my vision board is completed, I hang it on the wall in front of my desk.

Other methods of brainstorming your vision include creating an online vision board and setting it as your desktop picture or journaling it out in as much detail as possible.

Find your big hairy audacious goal (BHAG). 'What is the figure that *scares* you?'

I was sitting at Funnel Hacking Live in Orlando, Florida, a four-day conference for online business owners. On day three, one of the speakers asked this question. And it came as a shock to me that it startled me. I thought I had goal setting in the bag, but it struck me then that I wasn't daring to dream big enough. I had outlined some pretty boring, relatively easy goals that I knew that I could achieve if I wanted them enough. But what was the big-picture revenue? Why was I not thinking bigger?

The figure immediately came into my mind: £10,000,000. And as it entered my mind, judgement immediately entered too.

On the one hand, I was judging myself for thinking too small. 'Is that all? There are people in this room doing that per month.' On the other hand, I was questioning if I was really capable. As I sat with it, my gut told me that for now, £10m was right for me. It was the next milestone without having a massive team infrastructure or new premises.

The concept of the BHAG was first introduced to the world by Jim Collins and Jerry Porras via their visionary book *Built To Last*.[6] It is quite simply all about encouraging you to stop limiting your thinking. You're going to need to know your income BHAG for the next section, so I pose the same question to you:

What is the figure (financially) that scares you?

Please don't be influenced by mine. Yours might be smaller, it might be bigger, and it can also change over time. What is that figure right now for you? Try and choose with as little judgement on yourself possible. You're going to need to know your BHAG for our next exercise.

---

6   Collins, J; Porras, J *Built To Last: Successful habits of visionary companies* (Harper Business, 2011)

Goal Setting

Now that you've created your compelling vision (you should feel moved just thinking about it; I get goosebumps thinking about mine), let's work out the steps you need to take to achieve it. Something you'll learn about me over the coming chapters is that I like practical exercises; you won't find any fluff or 'BS' here on subjects like becoming a millionaire in the next few weeks.

Firstly, we've got to break down your financial BHAG into digestible bitesize chunks to be completed in a realistic timeframe. Let's look at how this worked for me.

The Results Of Goal Setting

In my first year of business, I was aimless. I had no direction. I was saying yes to anything and everything and the results spoke for themselves: I was struggling to create £1,000 per month in revenue.

That was until I wrote down my financial goals. At the time, goals seemed pointless as I could write them down, but I would have no clue on how to actually achieve them. But I got a large piece of card, printed off a pair of high heels and silhouettes of women along with a cityscape image and wrote 'The Vision'. I had even mixed up vision and goals. Then I wrote out my goals.

Short term: I wanted to achieve £1,500 in sales each month, so I wrote out the months from June to December.

Long term: I looked at the next few years and plucked some numbers from thin air as I had no gauge on what was possible:

- 2017: £18k

- 2018: £30k

- 2019: £40k

As I looked at my goals, I immediately felt over-whelmed and a bit stupid. I had never achieved over £1k in revenue in one month; how did I expect to all of a sudden generate £1.5k? And as I looked at 2018 with a revenue of £30k, I thought how impossible that sounded right now. But I tried not to judge too much and rolled with what I had written.

Little did I know how this exercise would change my life.

I pinned my goals to my bedroom wall and each day as I woke up, I asked myself, 'How do I move the business forward?' The number 1,500 was engrained in my brain. I set out to do everything I could to achieve it: attend as many networking events as possible; post on social media; ask current clients for referrals and so much more.

For the first time ever, that June, I earned £1,500. I was gobsmacked, I excitedly ran to my goal board and ticked the goal three times.

The next month, I did it again, this time actually beating my own goal. In July, I earned £1,600. And from there, I stopped ticking my goal board as I watched my income double, and then triple.

In 2018, I had a goal of turning over £30,000 in one year. This would go on to be the twelve-month period that my business would turn over seven figures.

How?

1. I had tapped in to the power of writing down achievable, measurable goals – the method I'm going to teach you within this chapter.

2. Looking at them and focusing on them every day, I asked the same question: 'How am I going to move the needle towards the goal?'

3. I used all of the marketing strategies and secrets I am sharing in this book and took action on them. Remember, *action* is imperative.

My Goal Setting Method

'I don't know how to earn 10k per month – I haven't even earned a penny.'

I was at a half-day business event and one of the speakers asked the audience to write down our ideal income (the equivalent of my revenue BHAG). I wrote 10k per month. The speaker then asked us to write an action list of how we were going to achieve that. I felt my face flush as I had no idea. I was currently earning zero in my business; I had no idea on how to leap to 10k per month.

Was 10k unachievable? Absolutely not. Was it an unrealistic short-term goal when my business was currently making no sales? Yes.

This is my issue with how most people teach you to set goals. If you set a short-term goal that feels unachievable to you, overwhelm will kick in and you'll either give in before trying or try, fail and feel disheartened. There is too big a gap between where you are right now and what you ultimately want to achieve. You need an in-between goal on the way to your dream income that is achievable and will build your confidence.

Think of your BHAG as the 'where you want to go' flag. As you can see, there is a gap that you need to fill. I like to think of a set of stairs crossing the gap, each stair representing a small milestone on the way to your large goal.

Insert your BHAG as your ultimate goal and work out the short-term goals along the road to get there, the first of which is known as your monthly survival budget.

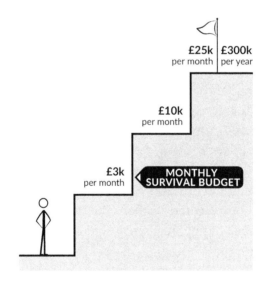

The example shows 300k (25k per month) as the BHAG broken into smaller short-term goals, the first goal being the monthly survival budget.

Your First Goal: Your Monthly Survival Budget

Whether you're currently employed and looking to ditch your day job or you're looking to launch your business as an additional income stream, your first goal is your monthly survival budget. This is the income you need to earn in order to survive. It is relatively easy to work out.

If you're currently employed, what monthly salary do you need to replace? If you don't have an income to replace, what essential outgoings do you need to cover (mortgage or rent, car payments, bills, groceries, etc)?

Once you've worked out your monthly survival budget, this is your *only* priority. Wake up daily and ask yourself how you're going to move the needle towards this goal. You can outline your larger short-term goals on the other steps of the diagram, but know that throughout our time together, your only goal is to replace your income so that you can go full time in your home-staging business if that is your goal.

Now that you are armed with a compelling vision that moves you and you have complete clarity on what you need to achieve, I'm excited to dive into the next steps with you and support you in launching your business.

Chapter Action List

There are a few actions you need to take to clarify your vision and your goals, remembering that the two are not the same thing. These include:

- Following the method set out in this chapter, create your vision board for your life and business.

- Write down your income BHAG.

- Draw the stair diagram and add your BHAG income to the top step.

- Work out your monthly survival budget and add it to your diagram.

- Put your monthly survival budget on display everywhere in your home and workspace to ensure it's always on your mind.

5

Reverse Engineer Your Dream Income

By now, you should be clear on the vision you have for your life and business. How exciting! You should also have a BHAG so scary you can't sleep and a more practical monthly survival budget figure. Is it engrained in your mind? Good. I want you to be obsessed with this number.

Now, it's time to get mathematical and apply a formula. Don't worry, this isn't going to be boring, quite the opposite. We're going to be talking about *money* – someone pass me a money gun!

I am passionate about coaching women on how to build home-staging businesses as I genuinely believe it is one of the best business models in the world. There are few models that allow you to:

- Scale an infinite amount of revenue with zero start-up funds

- Secure clients without any experience in the industry or prior design experience

- Do something you *love* every day while working significantly fewer days than you did in your nine to five

My main goal in this chapter is for you to know how many properties you need to stage each year to hit your income goal. Spoiler alert: it's not as many properties as you may think. Knowing this specific number will not only reduce the overwhelm you feel, but it will also keep you laser focused.

How To Start From Zero

As I explained in Chapter 1, I built my seven-figure home-staging business by using the 'Pay Before Install' method. This exact business model is what I will be sharing with you in this chapter. Using it, you will have the ability to scale your business to an infinite amount of revenue with no start-up money at all in the bank.

Let's recap what the Pay Before Install method looks like.

Client # 1:

- Your client pays you upfront for the installation: £2,000

- You then purchase the staging kit, costing £2,000

- Profit: 0

Remember, the key here is that you now own the kit and you have merely rented it to your client for six weeks. Meaning that when the rental period expires or your client requests that you remove the kit, you can move it to the next property you are staging. One staging kit is the furniture and accessories you require to fully stage a property.

Client # 2:

- Your client pays you upfront for the installation: £2,000

- You move the kit from the first property (spending 10% on moving it): £200

- Profit: £1,800

After two stages, from an investment of zero, your business is now in a profit of £1,800. Based on this example alone, within twelve months, from an investment of zero, your business will be in profit of £12,600. How? Let's do the maths.

First, let's work out how many times you can rent your kit in one year:

52 weeks/6-week rental period = 8.6

Answer: you can rent your kit eight times per year.

Let's break it down:

Stage	Income	Expenses	Bank Account
1	2,000	2,000	0
2	2,000	200	1,800
3	2,000	200	3,600
4	2,000	200	5,400
5	2,000	200	7,200
6	2,000	200	9,000
7	2,000	200	10,800
8	2,000	200	12,600

This example is based on you working only eight days per year. At ThePropertyStagers, we advise our clients that their property will be staged within twenty-four hours, even though it now only takes the team a few hours to set everything up. However, I would calculate longer than a few hours if you are just starting out.

Why is home staging one of the best business models in the world?

If I put £1 into the bank, my return is currently likely to be around £1.06 per year. If I put £1 into home staging, my return is £12,600 per year. I don't know about you, but I'm choosing home staging.

Before we go any further, I'm sure you have some questions you'd like answered. Here are a few I get asked regularly.

Q: Why are you charging the removal of the kit at 10% of the fee?

A: It's impossible for me to give an exact figure for each reader, but 10% is the standard fee I would pay to have a kit moved from location A to B.

Q: What about the cost of kit storage?

A: In this example, I am not including monthly expenses as it is not possible for me to calculate this for your personal circumstance. However, what I can say is that your monthly outgoings when you launch your home-staging business are very low. You will likely not need storage as there are creative methods to avoid it, but if you do, it is a relatively low cost. For the first two years of my business, for a 100sqft storage unit, my cost was £140 per month.

Q: What if the second property isn't the same size as the first?

A: This is an example scenario. I have worked this out based on my price example of 2k, but it could also work out even more lucrative if the next property I stage has a higher invoice value.

When you're working out a calculation for your own circumstances, base it on the lowest price you will charge. You do not want to sugar-coat the results.

Q: Why is the rental period six weeks?

A: I have tested different rental periods (both longer and shorter) and in my experience, I have found six weeks to be the sweet spot.

Q: What if there is a period that I don't have the kit rented?

A: With the marketing methods I'm going to teach you, it is unlikely this will be the case.

Now let's look at the most frequently asked question of them all.

What If I Want To Charge More?

I've based my example on a 2k charge for a two-bedroom property, but it is possible that in your area, the average you could charge is a lot higher than my example. My company has staged properties for £2,000–£20,000, depending on the size, location and price point of the property.

To make it simple for you, in this section, I have included the calculations for a 3k and 5k example.

3K Example

Installation	Income	Expenses	Bank Account
1	3,000	3,000	0
2	3,000	300	2,700
3	3,000	300	5,400
4	3,000	300	8,100
5	3,000	300	10,800
6	3,000	300	13,500
7	3,000	300	16,200
8	3,000	300	18,900

5K Example

Installation	Income	Expenses	Bank Account
1	5,000	5,000	0
2	5,000	500	4,500
3	5,000	500	9,000
4	5,000	500	13,500
5	5,000	500	18,000
6	5,000	500	22,500
7	5,000	500	27,000
8	5,000	500	31,500

Now that we've worked out how much you can earn with just one kit in one year, let's take a look at how many properties you need to stage to earn your desired monthly income.

The Reverse Engineer Formula

1. Work out your yearly survival budget

The first step is to work out your yearly survival budget by applying this formula:

Your monthly survival budget × 12
= Yearly survival budget

For example, if my monthly survival budget is £2,000 per month, I will multiply it by twelve, which equals £24,000 per year.

2. Work out the average price

The next step of the formula is to look at the average price you will charge. As our community of #Stager-Boss students is based all over the world, I can't advise you specifically on what you can charge in your area. For you to work out this figure, I'm going to give you a brief guide. However, if you would like to take this a step further, then I suggest that you do market research in your area to discover the low, mid and high end of the market.

For this formula, you are going to work out what end of the market you would like to position yourself at. One quote from my business journey that has always stuck in my mind and I've followed is from the grandfather of marketing, Dan Kennedy:

'There is no strategic advantage of being the second lowest-price leader in town, but there is huge strategic advantage of being the most expensive.'[7]

What this says to me is that there is only an advantage to being the *most* expensive company on the market. I'd like to take this quote further and suggest that there is a huge advantage in being the *least* expensive. If you're anywhere in between, you'll be overlooked and forgotten.

Think this through: if you're sourcing a service provider, you'll receive a handful of quotes and it's likely you'll choose the least expensive or the most expensive. The quotes in the middle that are all of a similar value are easily overlooked. So, the question is: which end of the spectrum will you fall into? There is no right or wrong answer; it depends on the service you want to offer and the client you want to serve.

When you're considering which price point you'll position yourself at, remember this: if you choose to charge a high price, expect a low volume of work, and if you charge a low price, expect to do a high volume. Think of handbags. The more expensive a handbag is, the fewer will sell. A designer brand will sell thousands of one handbag while a large discount-store retailer will likely sell hundreds of

---

7   Kennedy, DS *No BS Marketing to the Affluent: No holds barred, take no prisoners guide to getting really rich* (3rd Edition, Gildan Media, 2019)

thousands of one bag. Which end of the market are you going to position yourself?

Depending on your decision, I suggest setting your average price based on this example. It in turn is based on the industry average charge for a two-bedroom property.

Low End	Mid End	High End
2k	3k	5k

If you know in your area that there are only five-bedroom villas worth 1 m+, your low-end price could be 5k. If you're based in an area where a four-bedroom house sells for 75k, your high-end price could be 3k. Depending on your location, you may want to base your formula on a completely different set of figures; the ones I have given are simply examples.

3. Use the 8 Installation Calculation

The final step to the Reverse Engineer Formula, the 8 Installation Calculation, is going to help you to work out how many properties you'll need to stage per year to earn your desired income. In the three tables coming up:

- **Kit** refers to how many kits you need to own

- **Stages** refer to how many properties you need to stage each year

- **Profit** is how much profit you would make if you were to stage X number of properties per year

So, how do you use the 8 Installation Calculation?

1. Having chosen which price you are going to base your average charge on, 2k, 3k or 5k, go to the relevant table.

2. Scan the right-hand column for the figure that is closest to your yearly survival budget.

3. Look at the kit and stages column. This will indicate how many properties you need to stage each year and how many kits you would need to own to do so.

Then write out your statement: 'I need to stage X properties per year in order to earn my desired income of Y.' How many properties do you need to stage per year?

2K Example

Kit	No of Stages	Profit
1	8	12,600
2	16	25,200
3	24	37,800
4	32	50,400
5	40	63,000

3K Example

Kit	Stages	Profit
1	8	18,900
2	16	37,800
3	24	56,700
4	32	75,600
5	40	94,500

5K Example

Kit	Stages	Profit
1	8	31,500
2	16	63,000
3	24	94,500
4	32	126,000
5	40	157,500

Please note: the profit increases on your second year as you don't need to calculate the cost for the kit again in your first sale.

If you would like to work out the 8 Installation Calculation based on your own average price, the formula is:

(7 × [Average price]) – 10%
= Profit for one year with 1 kit (8 stages)

I want to make this as simple as possible for you, so instead of working this out in your head, I've designed the 'Reverse Engineer Calculator'. All you have to do is input your information and the formula will work it out for you. Visit StagerBossTheBook.com/bonus for your calculator, along with additional content and resources to support you on your home-staging journey.

Isn't it mind-blowing? And may I remind you that however many properties you need to stage, that is how many days you need to work *in* your business per year to create that income. Of course, you'll need to work other days *on* your business: admin, marketing, finances. But wow! If you are a full-time employee, you'll currently work around 261 days per year. You could reduce your working days by a huge amount.

You can now see why home staging is one of the best business models in the world. And you can do *all* of it without investing any of your own money.

Earning your monthly survival budget could be closer than you think. Now you know how many properties you need to stage, I'd like to highlight that I have used the word *properties*, not *clients*. What if I told you that you could earn your yearly income with just one client? One client could give you all of the properties for the year. And it's not uncommon. I've done the maths.

At ThePropertyStagers, 76% of our clients stage more than one property with us. One client staged a block of 169 apartments with us; another client renovates three properties per month and always stages with us. In Chapter 7, I'm going to share with you how to find those clients. They are what I like to call game-changer clients.

However, we have work to do before we get there. In the next chapter, I'm going to share with you the potential services you can offer.

Chapter Action List

The actions you need to take on the back of the knowledge you have gained from this chapter include:

- Work out your yearly survival budget.

- Decide where you would like to position yourself in the market.

- Choose your example average price.

- Use the 8 Installation Calculation.

- Write your statement: 'I need to stage X properties per year to earn my desired income'.

6

Choose Your Signature Service

One hundred and eighty-two drawers.

I'll always remember the day vividly. I had been in business for nine months and a property developer client had asked if I designed and furnished offices. My ambition kicked in (it does that; it's both a curse and a blessing) and I wanted the commission, so I said, 'Yes, of course I do.'

The invoice was sent off the next day with the installation booked for the following week. But the installation didn't go to plan. I had never furnished an office before and my suppliers didn't offer the furniture I was looking for within the budget. It ended up being a time-consuming and stressful process, sourcing what I needed. Secondly, as I didn't know the new suppliers, I had no leverage to ask for a discount and preferential delivery times. And, of course, the order didn't turn up on time. Finally, I was unfamiliar with the products. I didn't realise all of the furniture would come flat-packed – including the 182 drawers. It took a nineteen-hour shift to complete the office. I was exhausted and there was very little profit in the installation.

The issue? This was not my signature service.

This is the reason that most people aren't successful: they have shiny-object syndrome – like I did in this example. A sexy new business opportunity comes along and they say yes. Often, this 'sexy business opportunity' is the temptation to offer a service that they don't usually offer just to make a sale. To put it bluntly, this is the fastest way to your business failing.

In the example above, saying yes to a service that wasn't in my wheelhouse just to get business cost me time, money, energy and, more importantly, it distracted me from securing business that I wanted: business that could actually make me money. There is only one way to avoid being a serial 'yes person', but it's going to require discipline and following your own rules, which for entrepreneurs can be challenging.

The solution: *Choose a signature service.*

What is your signature service? This is the service that will be at the centre of all your marketing and sales messaging until you've become the undisputed go-to expert in your area. When someone mentions your service, your name should be the first to come up, almost like a reflex.

Your Signature Service Options

When choosing your signature service, you will need to consider many things, eg, how many hours you want to work, how much income you want/require and how it fits into your lifestyle goals. There will be a particular service that immediately piques your interest more than the others, but I suggest you keep an open mind and consider all options before deciding the best fit for you and your income goals.

Be warned if you choose to ignore this advice and offer all of the services. There is nothing I hate more than coming across someone online and they are a home stager, interior designer, property sourcer, property investor, cleaner, coach and speaker. It immediately screams that they have no expertise in anything.

Choose *one* niche and stick to it. It takes time to become the go-to expert; it will not happen overnight. As I promised at the start of the book, I don't give advice unless I've personally implemented it myself. I didn't offer a different service to my signature service for eighteen months and I didn't start building a second business until I was four years into my entrepreneurial journey (when I already owned my seven-figure home-staging business).

Stay focused. Let's look at the different services you can offer.

Service 1: Staging For Sale: Vacant Properties

This is the signature service that was the foundation of my business. In fact, I scaled my business to seven figures mainly providing this service, so I've got you if this is your choice. This for me really is the definition of home staging: taking an empty space and completely transforming it to be market ready.

What this service looks like:

- The client will rent your kit of furniture/staging items for a period of time until they request that the kit is removed or the property sells.

- The business owns the kits and rents them out to the client.

Some clients may not want to rent the kit, but purchase it instead, and it is your choice whether to offer this service (it's great when you want to replace your stock). You may also offer the option that at the end of the rental period, the buyer can purchase the kit. Quite often, the person who has bought the property wants all of the items.

Which business owner is this signature service perfect for?

- Someone with no start-up funds. This was the exact strategy I used to start ThePropertyStagers with no funds, as shared in Chapter 5.

- Someone who wants to build an empire. You can scale to as many kits and clients as you'd like, and an infinite revenue. You are in control.

- Someone who wants a lifestyle business. As you control the growth of the company, one to two kits could keep you busy a couple of days per month.

The benefits:

- **No upfront investment required.** I encourage all of my coaching students to take payment upfront, meaning they can purchase the goods with the client's money and make an immediate profit.

- **Long-term profitability.** Once the initial investment is made into the stock, you can continue to make income from the same kit for years to come.

- **Control.** With this structure, you keep control of how big you want to grow your business. You can decide to buy more stock to fulfil orders or press pause.

- **Structure to scale.** Given you can control your speed of growth, you can decide to have the capacity to fulfil fifty stages or five.

- **Creativity.** As you will purchase the kit, you decide on your look and what your client will receive.

- **You can grow without risk.** Given you are paid before purchasing stock, you can grow quickly.

The downfalls:

- **Higher-risk strategy than other options.** As much as you can control the speed of growth of your company, there may be a risk that from time to time, you don't have clients, which means your stock isn't always making you money.

- **Not having the right team or systems.** At any given time, ThePropertyStagers will be responsible for relocating twenty to thirty kits per month for staging, which is logistically challenging. You must have the right team / systems around you if you'd like to scale.

- **Higher outgoings than other options.** The more properties you stage, naturally, the more your outgoings will increase to service the demand. Team, storage and vehicles mean you need to scale your backend as you scale your sales.

Service 2: Occupied Home Staging
Or House Doctoring

This may be your initial impression of home staging as it is the one made famous by many TV shows. This is where a company will enter the homeowner's residence and give it a makeover, usually because it is for sale.

While this service isn't a large part of my company strategy, it is one that we have offered. It can be perfect for the new business owner or someone who is more cautious about getting into the business as you will require less furniture than staging for sale, and therefore, lower investment. However, it doesn't give you the same creative control or scalability as vacant home staging.

What this service looks like:

- You are usually working on the client's residence, so they will either live with the items or pack them away (eg bedding/linen, etc) until the property is being viewed.

- You supply styling accessories (and/or furniture) for the client's property, often working with some of their own personal items and some of your staging items.

- The items may be rented or purchased by the client.

Which business owner is this signature service perfect for?

- Someone with no start-up funds. The stock you require for offering this service is dramatically less than to stage a vacant property. Also, just like staging a vacant property for sale, you can structure this as a payment upfront deal.

- Someone who wants a lifestyle business. With little stock to hold, many operators will run their business from home and stage a few days per month.

- Someone who is cautious about starting a business. As there is little commitment to stock, storage space, vehicles and staff, you can start as soon as possible.

The benefits:

- **Profit for little stock.** Once the initial investment is made into stock, you can continue to make income from the same kit for years.

- **Little investment upfront.** With this structure, you keep control of how big you want to grow your business. You can decide to buy more stock to fulfil orders or press pause.

The downfalls:

- **You never know how much stock is required.** As you don't know the type or style of property you will stage, it can be a challenge to cater for varying types of home.

- **Challenging to match the client's taste/style.** There is a world of possibilities in terms of the style of the client's property and taste. You will most definitely need to see images of the property before staging.

- **You're working in someone's home.** When you're staging a property that the client lives in and their personal items are in the home, it can be a challenge to persuade them to remove certain items.

- **Lack of scalability.** Not ideal if you want to scale a large and profitable business.

Service 3: Serviced Accommodation (SA), Houses Of Multiple Occupancy (HMOs), Student Accommodation Or Long-Term Rentals

Once we had mastered staging for sale and become the nation's industry leaders for this service, the next flagship service for ThePropertyStagers was staging for rental accommodation. We have now developed our own furniture range that we manufacture ourselves.

Don't worry – you don't have to manufacture your own furniture, suppliers will suffice. But it all needs to be in line with your vision, remember.

Firstly, I'll clear up what the terminology in the heading means:

- **SA** is a short rental property such as a holiday or corporate rental. Think of an Airbnb listing.

- An **HMO** is a large property with rooms that tenants can individually rent.

- **Student accommodation** could be student apartments or halls of residence.

- **Long-term rentals** means providing furniture for properties rented long term, usually buy-to-lets (BTLs).

What this service looks like:

- Your client will purchase everything in the property as it will be getting used by the tenants.

- For all of these services, but SAs mainly, you usually need to provide the furniture and/or everything else that someone needs to live in the property.

- You will be kitting out a full house, which means furniture. For SA, you will need to include crockery, TV, bedding, bathroom items, etc in addition to furniture.

- You will provide functional high-quality goods as there will be high footfall in these properties.

Which business owner is this signature service perfect for?

- **Someone with no start-up funds.** You will charge your client upfront, purchase the kit and build in a profit margin, hence you can scale this business model from zero.

- **Someone who is looking to scale big.** If you use a company to manufacture and deliver the furniture, there is very little outlay required by you.

- **Someone who is looking for full-time work.** As this type of project is a longer process than staging for sale, it is perfect for someone prepared to invest time.

- **Someone who is in an area where 'homes sell anyway'.** Every home stager's most hated statement. An estate agent or client will sometimes claim that their home will sell without staging. If you are in an area that is non-receptive to the concept of home staging, consider specialising in this service.

- **Someone who is in a heavily populated student or holiday-rental area.** If you are based in a university or college area, a major city or a tourist destination, you will find many clients who are desperate for your help with this service.

The benefits:

- **This service is necessary.** Your client cannot rent their property (SA, HMO or student) without furniture, meaning your service is necessary, unlike staging for sale which is someone's choice.

- **No upfront investment required.** I encourage all of my coaching students to take payment upfront, meaning they can purchase the goods with the client's money and make an instant profit.

- **High profit.** This is one of the easiest strategies to build in profit.

- **Chance to shake up inventory.** As you will constantly be selling the inventory you put into a property, you will have the chance to change up your look with every property.

- **You can grow without risk.** As you are paid before purchasing stock, you can grow quickly.

The downfalls:

- **Labour intensive.** As you are not only furnishing what is on show, but also what is in the kitchen cupboards, on the beds, etc, each project takes more energy and possibly several people to complete if you don't engage a company to at least deliver the furniture, stock the kitchen, etc. ThePropertyStagers offers this service to many independent home-staging companies. This takes the strain out of the installation, leaving the home stager to stage the property, ie, do the nice bit.

- **Competitive marketplace.** You are often competing with furniture giants and superstores.

- **Time-consuming.** Talking with clients, quoting, supplying – every part of the process takes longer than the other options.

- **Constant inventory overhaul.** As fun as it is constantly buying new stock, it can become challenging in terms of maintaining stock, availability and continuity in style.

Service 4: Virtual Staging

This is not a service we offer at ThePropertyStagers. It is, however, a service you can potentially offer in your home-staging business.

If this is the service that calls out to you, I suggest that it will only ever be your sole service as virtual staging will cannibalise your other services. That's why we do not offer it at ThePropertyStagers. For example, if you suggest that a client stages their property for sale and the price is 5k, but you also offer virtual staging for 10% of what it would cost to physically stage the property, your client is likely going to be inclined to go with the cheaper option.

One of the common fears is 'But what if someone asks for it?' In this case, you have two options:

1. Recommend a fellow home-staging company that offers virtual home staging. You are not missing out on any business by doing this because it's not a service you offer.

2. Explain the benefits of physically staging a property versus virtually staging a property, specifically highlighting that a viewer would be disappointed upon viewing the empty property that it doesn't look like the photos. This is the reasoning I always present.

What this service looks like:

- Your client provides you with images and measurements of the empty property space and you virtually stage it using a program or software.

Which business owner is this signature service perfect for?

- Someone who wants a lifestyle business. As you don't need to leave your home, this service could work perfectly alongside your current business or career.

- Someone who wants to work remotely. If you're looking for a business that you can run from anywhere, you could virtually stage any property in the world from anywhere in the world.

- Someone who is tech savvy. As virtual staging is 'virtual', a basic level of tech skills will be required.

The benefits:

- **No upfront investment required.** I encourage all of my coaching students to take payment upfront, meaning you can purchase the tech you will need with the client's money and make a profit.

- **You can grow without risk**. There is no physical element to this business, apart from you, wifi and a laptop, so the running costs are very low.

The downfalls:

- **Labour intensive.** This service may not be physically intense, but it is a labour-intensive process to virtually stage a property.

- **Requires a new skill.** You will likely have to study a new platform or software.

- **Low ticket.** Virtual staging doesn't carry a big price tag, so you will need to secure a high volume of clients to earn your desired income.

There is no right or wrong answer when it comes to selecting the service that you would like to specialise in, but I suggest you choose the one that is aligned with your vision and goals. Choosing one service may feel like a challenge, but I'm a big believer in the saying 'jack of all trades, master of none'. The logistics of offering a staging-for-sale service compared to an SA/HMO service – two services in the same genre – are completely different.

When you've chosen a signature service, there are going to be other shiny opportunities along your journey that will distract you from going for gold. Not only is it important that you become the go-to expert for your niched service, it's also key that you don't offer bolt-on services to generate additional income.

One of my most frequently asked questions from students is 'My client has asked me if I offer X, should I just say yes?' This often refers to cleaning services, project management, bespoke curtains, painting and decorating, etc. The answer to this question is always a resounding no. Time spent cleaning the property or becoming a part-time decorator is time away from working on your business and finding an ideal client that could multiply your income tenfold.

You might feel afraid of saying no to your client when they ask if you offer additional services as we're often taught that the customer is always right. Know that most of the time, this will not impact your relationship negatively, but positively as you will gain more respect from them when you tell them you like to focus on what you are an expert in. I know this is easier said than done, especially when you're starting out, but when you step into your power and your expertise, this will position you at number one with your client and draw them to working with you.

Now that you've chosen your signature service, let's look at who your dream client would be. That's what is coming up in the next chapter.

Chapter Action List

There's not a lot on the action list for this chapter, but there is still action you must take. That is quite simply:

• Choose your signature service and stick with it until you become the go-to expert.

7

Game-Changing Clients: Who Are They And How Do You Find Them?

'Let's go ahead.'

I'll never forget the day when this email popped up in my inbox. My dream client had just agreed to move ahead with a £260,000 quote. It's the day that everything changed.

Let me take you back. My first interaction with this exact same client wasn't as positive as it appears now. He had contacted me twelve months prior, asking for a quote to furnish a two-bedroom apartment for SA. The quote was roughly £5k and he came back and said that it was too expensive. At the time, I felt deflated and a little annoyed as I had actually spent a lot of time on him, emailing back and forth regarding his requirements. But it's just part of business and as always, I moved on to the next quote and client.

Around twelve months later, a DM dropped into my Facebook inbox and it was his name that popped up. I'll confess, I was sceptical as I read the message:

> 'Hi, Liv, I've been following you online since we last spoke and I'm really impressed. I've just taken on a block of forty-five apartments in London, would you be able to provide a quote?'

If I was too expensive for one apartment, I would be too expensive for forty-five! However, as we went back and forth again via email, I started to input into my pricing calculator the quantity of each item. . . 90 x double beds; 45 x three-seater sofas; 180 dining chairs, etc. The quote came out at £260,000.

I remember the moment so vividly as I showed the screen to my mum. We were sitting next to each other in our home office and we both burst out laughing. It seemed so inconceivable that this installation would actually go ahead, but I hit send on the email and my quote was sent.

Even when we got the green light, it felt surreal. . . until the money was deposited into our bank account over a period of two weeks. This client was financing this forty-five apartment installation with various lenders, so the money came in in 45–90k amounts from different funders. Then the chaos of manufacturing and ordering everything we needed began.

I flew to London from my home in Spain for the two weeks of the installation and stayed in the block of forty-five apartments alongside my brother (who worked for me at the time), my mum and our other team members. No, we didn't take an apartment each; my mum and I shared (as always). It was actually quite spooky, staying in an empty block, and trust me: you do not want to lose your phone in one of forty-five identical apartments. I know from experience.

Why am I sharing this with you? There are a few lessons to take away from this story:

- Your dream client is out there and this is the chapter where I'm going to show you how to identify and find them.

- Just because someone says no, it may only mean no for now. Any client can come back and work with you in the future. It is absolutely key to leave every potential client with a positive experience, even if they have rejected your quote.

- This client came back because I was consistently showing up online daily. He was watching (although I didn't know it at the time) and when it came to deciding who he would work with to furnish his block of apartments, it was me who was on his mind, not anyone else.

Here's the thing: I could tell you many stories like this because I've made it a habit to seek out and attract my ideal clients. I could tell you about the block of 169 apartments that ThePropertyStagers furnished or the estate agent who passes us more than twenty-five properties per year to stage or another ten clients I can think of off the top of my head who have trusted us with multiple blocks.

I call these game-changing clients, simply because they can change the game for your business. They have for me. This forty-five-apartment block was the turning point in my business and helped it reach seven figures. Not only do dream clients boost your bank account, but they instil confidence in you as the business owner and in other potential clients who see how capable you are of handling large instal-lations. Market these successes and it will attract more clients.

The question is, how do you find game-changing cli-ents? The first and most important step is to identify who your ideal client is. It will be different for every-one, depending on what service you are offering and the goals that you have for your business. This isn't just about understanding the demographics, but the psychographics too. You want to know your client better than they know themselves (creepy, I know, but it works).

Demographics

The demographics of your ideal client are going to give you insight into *who* it is you are targeting. This is incredibly important when it comes to marketing: if you know who you are marketing to, you can work out where this person will spend time both online and offline. For example, if I'm targeting a young demographic of under twenty-ones, they will spend their time on different platforms to the over forty-fives.

Fortunately, having been in this industry for a long time, I'm not only going to guide you on what you need to know; I'm going to give you my own personal insights and data. Let's start by building your ideal-client avatar:

- **Age.** From my own experience and data, your ideal client's age is likely going to range from twenty-five to sixty-four. ThePropertyStagers carried out a study on Google Ads and noticed that nobody under the age of twenty-four or over sixty-five had enquired to use our service.

- **Gender.** I was excited to launch #StagerBoss as our ideal-client avatar is a woman and I love all things female empowerment. With ThePropertyStagers, the gender was different: 80%+ of our clients are male. The property industry is male dominated and we've found that men are happier to outsource the interiors side of things, while women often opt to do it themselves.

- **Location.** Consider whether your ideal client is located close to their property or are they remote? Targeting remote investors can be a good idea as they have no other option but to pay for a service like yours; they are not close enough to do it themselves.

- **Occupation/role.** I have detailed below the potential careers of your dream client, based on your signature service. Your ideal client will always be a decision maker within their company. My most successful relationships have been with the CEO/business owner, who can implement company-wide initiatives and make decisions fast.

  - Vacant staging for sale/virtual home staging: property investor or developer, house builder, estate agent, development company, homeowner

  - Occupied home staging: homeowner, estate agent

  - SA/HMO/student and rental: SA operator, HMO landlord, BTL landlord, student accommodation operator, holiday-let management agency, short-term rental agency

Brainstorm exactly who your ideal client is. Even give them a name so that you can humanise them. I love this example from John Lee Dumas, the host of the *Entrepreneur On Fire* podcast.[8] His avatar for the podcast is called 'Jimmy' and every decision he makes when it comes to deciding on the direction of the podcast, he runs through 'What would Jimmy do?'

An example dream client avatar:

- **Name:** David.

- **Age:** Thirty-five to forty.

- **Gender:** Male.

- **Occupation/role:** David is the owner of an estate agency with three branches across the local area. He and his team have won a few awards for their service and are very involved in the community.

A few key things to highlight in this example:

- David is the owner (key decision maker).

- There are three branches of his agency. This indicates it is an independent/small business (easier to target these than corporate companies as decisions can be made quickly and rolled out company-wide).

- The awards indicate that the business is successful, but be aware of its image. David

---

8   Dumas, JL 'Meet Jimmy: He'll tell you all about EntrepreneurOnFire!' (YouTube, 2012) www.youtube.com/watch?v=YUQY1XKWB2I

and his team will likely be open to listing good-looking staged properties for sale.

- The company is heavily involved in the local community, so may be active on social-media groups you can become part of or in events you can attend.

Demographics are extremely valuable as not only can you now picture your ideal client and gain some knowledge of what their life looks like, you can also determine where your ideal client spends time. However, knowing where they are and actually being able to get their attention are two separate things. When you truly understand the psychographics of your ideal clients, what drives and motivates them, you can throw hooks out online and offline that they are likely to take notice of.

Psychographics

You may be feeling at this moment like this section is overkill. 'Liv,' you may ask, 'do I really need to know my ideal client inside out? Isn't it as simple as they want to sell their property more quickly and for more money than they would without my services?' While yes, this is likely the ultimate desire of your dream client, if you can make that client feel you understand them more than any other brand or company, then they're going to work with you over any of your competitors.

Many times in business, I have tried to fast track this process by thinking I already know my ideal client and unfortunately, it has seriously impacted my results. One example was when I was recording episodes for the #StagerBoss podcast. They were long episodes, around sixty minutes each, and I wasn't seeing the monthly listens that I wanted.

When I returned to the drawing board and really got crystal clear on who my ideal client is, I realised that she doesn't have time to sit and listen to sixty-minute episodes; she wants a download of all things staging to listen to while she is busy living her normal life. She's listening to the podcast while she's on the school run, putting washing in the machine or tidying up after the kids go to bed.

And so, I pivoted our strategy and started to record twenty-minute episodes with a juicy takeaway in each episode. Voila! It worked. #StagerBoss doubled its monthly podcast listens and now many people in our community message to share the lightbulb moments they've had while on the go.

Being inside your ideal client's head is the most invaluable marketing tool of all. From my example, you can see that by understanding my client's schedule, I had an impact on the podcast results. This is how granular you want to get, so let's get started.

The two most powerful ideal-client psychographics for you to study are their:

- Aspirations (goals, dreams, desires)

- Pain points

Every purchasing decision we make (that's everyone, including you and I) either moves us towards pleasure or away from pain. And even the same decision can be driven by a different need. For example, you're reading this book as you want to launch your home-staging business, but you'll likely find one of these statements more empowering than the other:

- You can launch your business and fire your boss (move away from pain).

- You can launch your business and finally be in control of your destiny (move towards pleasure).

Communicating a mixture of both pleasure and pain points will ensure that you are hitting all bases in your marketing messages to include every person in your audience, no matter their driver.

What Your Client Wants

Before I go into the details of your client's aspirations and pain points, I want to highlight the focus of your marketing message. It should be focused on the client and not your product or service. The mistake that most people in business make is they focus heavily on the outcome of their service rather than how it will fulfil their client's desires.

Give them what they want, sell them what they need.

What does this mean? News alert: you are not selling home staging. No one wakes up in the morning and the first thing they think is 'I would like to buy a staging package today.' Literally no one on this planet has ever done this, so why as business owners are we so desperate to keep pushing our services? What people do want is a solution that will move them away from pain or towards pleasure, and your service is the answer. In this scenario, it is home staging, but it could be anything else as long as it provides that solution.

Let me give you an example. My ideal client at #StagerBoss wants to quit her job as she is really unfulfilled (ie move away from pain). So I'm offering her a solution to leave her job by launching a home-staging business:

> *[Giving her what she wants – a chance to leave her unfulfilling job] = [Selling her what she needs – my course]*

My marketing message for #StagerBoss now becomes: 'Do you wanna ditch the day job and do something you love?' rather than 'Do you want to buy a home-staging business course?' No one wants to buy a course; they buy it because of the result.

They could get what they want through various other methods. They could launch an e-commerce business or a clothing brand. I attract them with my message, and then educate them on why launching a home-staging business is the best business model. Make sense?

Your client wants to earn as much money as possible from their property, and you and I both know that staging will maximise their profit on every deal, but they could also get their needs met if they reduced their costs or purchased more properties or adopted a new strategy. It is our job to hook them in with what they want and help educate them on why our service will help.

For ThePropertyStagers, the message is 'Do you want to sell your property quickly so that you can move on to your new property deal?' not 'Here is why home staging is great. . .'

Your Client's Aspirations

Now that you know all of your messaging has to have your ideal client in mind, let's break down your client's aspirations, also known as their goals, dreams and desires. Firstly, let's look at an example of their surface goals:

- They want to sell/rent their property as quickly as possible.

- They want the highest price possible.

- They want to increase the value and quality of their portfolio.

But there is something deeper within them, a reason they want all of the above, and it will be different depending on your ideal client. Here are a few examples:

- To provide for themselves and their family
- To build a business and legacy they are proud of
- To be recognised as the leader in their industry
- To earn more money fast so they can leave a job they hate
- To spend more time with their family

When you are able to get to the core of why your client requires your services, you can connect with them on a deeper than surface level. Remember, connection and understanding are what sells.

Your Client's Pain Points

If you can explain your client's pain points clearly enough, they'll automatically assume you have the solution to their problems. I don't know about you, but I've purchased programmes and courses because the person selling them speaks right to my soul; they know the exact pain I'm feeling right now and have articulated it so clearly that I don't care what it is they're selling, I'm buying.

Make your clients feel heard. Forget about a portfolio or experience; when a client feels like you understand them more than anyone else, they'll be sold.

What are the pain points of your ideal clients?

- What annoys or angers them? Eg, going over budget; a refurb taking longer than anticipated; obtaining planning permission.

- Do you have any common pain points?
  Eg, estate agents wanting to reduce the property price; builders letting you down. When you share a common 'enemy' with someone, you build connection.

- How are they struggling? Eg, their property won't sell; they need to sell this property quickly to move on to their next deal; they've overspent and need to maximise the profit; they don't have any time as they're so busy managing their business.

Brainstorming your client's pain points will help you in your marketing messaging online. It will also help in your conversations with potential clients, creating the 'you are in my head' effect. Highlighting your client's pain and pleasure points is incredibly power-ful, but the secret is to highlight both equally so that you're covering all bases, because some of your clients will respond more to solving their pain rather than fuelling their aspirations, and vice versa.

Now that you're getting to know your client inside out, the final part of the process is to create your client transformation statement. This is going to be a one-sentence statement that clearly indicates to clients how you serve them. Think of this like your elevator pitch.

Your Client Transformation Statement

This makes it crystal clear to your ideal client what problem your service solves. There are two steps to building it.

1. Your A to B Transformation is what your client's journey will look like when they're working with you. A = where they are now: struggling with their pain points and open to move to B. B = where they will be after they've worked with you/your product.

For example, A: my client's property is about to go on the market and they want the highest price possible.

B: my client's property sold for 20% above the valuation. They are delighted as they get to move on to their next deal quickly as a result.

When writing your A to B statement, be as specific as possible with the client's current position and the results of working with you.

2. Create your statement. It's time to fill in the blanks of your client transformation statement. For example:

> Hey, I'm / we are [Name of Company] and
> I / we help [Who – Ideal Client] go from [A]
> to [B].

For example:

> Hey, I'm Liv and I help ambitious women go
> from feeling unfulfilled and under-appreciated
> in their nine-to-fives to launching their home-
> staging businesses and claiming their time
> to shine.

Or:

> Hey, we are ThePropertyStagers and we
> help property developers go from feeling
> overwhelmed at the idea of furnishing a block
> of apartments to feeling stress-free as their
> apartments are professionally furnished and
> fully booked in days.

Your A to B Transformation statement will come in handy when you are networking and someone asks what you do, and on your social-media profiles. I especially recommend adding this to your bios.

Chapter Action List

This has been one of the most crucial chapters in the book. Why? Knowing your ideal client will propel your marketing message forward and convert leads.

Here's what you need to do next. As always, action is key to success:

- Create your dream client avatar.

- Write a list of your client's aspirations (their goals, dreams and desires).

- Write a list of your client's pain points.

- Create your client transformation statement.

8

Brand Your Business Like A Boss

'What if people don't know who I am anymore?'

It was a decision that I agonised over for weeks. I was a full year into my entrepreneurial journey and running what was at the time called 'LIVinteriors'. I could sense something wasn't landing with my brand, but I also feared that if I changed the name of the business, people wouldn't know who I was anymore. I'm laughing as I type this now – oh, hindsight.

This was the issue with my branding:

I was priming my business's audience for a different service.

Interior design and home staging are two very separate services, and so the expectations from clients differ for each. With interior design, a client usually receives a tailored and unique service specific to their brief and tastes. Home staging is different: you are designing a space for a mass market and staging the home to appeal to the buyers, not your client's taste. So when I was quoting for business, clients expected to have their taste taken into consideration. Staging does the opposite as it's pretty much a 'hands off' service for clients.

There were other problems with my mixed-up branding:

- **Wrong price tag.** If you add the word 'interiors' to the brand of your home-staging business, the perception in a client's mind is that you are expensive. They therefore perceive you as more expensive than your competitors. Now remember that you are usually staging an investment property or someone's home to sell, but it's not for them. They aren't going to want to spend as much money as they would on interior design because they will not be living in it and enjoying it. Be careful with your wording or you may be ruling yourself out as an option for your ideal client before you even reach the point of consultation.

- **Hard to spell.** There are many variations on how you could spell LIVinteriors, lessening the chance of my audience and clients finding me. It may actually have led them to a competitor.

- **The industry was 'unknown'.** At the time I was launching my home-staging business, most people didn't even know what home staging was. The industry is still in its infancy, which requires us as a community to raise the awareness of our service. In terms of a company name choice, 'doing what it says on the tin' is often the best way forward.

So, I decided to rebrand. I created a video that would pan over the LIVinteriors logo. There would be a sound effect and ThePropertyStagers logo would appear with some background music accompanying my masterpiece.

As I prepared for the big day when I would unveil the rebrand, I got nervous. What if my £30k-per-year business suddenly lost all of its clients? I anxiously pressed publish on my video and waited to watch the craziness unfold before me.

Hours passed. . . one hour. . . two hours. . . eight hours. My post had a few likes and no comments. I panicked that people were not happy, but instead, what I found out was that people didn't care. And in this moment, I realised that I cared more about my brand, my business (my baby) than anyone else.

It might seem a little counterintuitive in a chapter about branding where I'm telling you people don't care. I don't mean it quite as literally as it sounds. People do care, but only if you've built a household brand, which at the time, I most certainly hadn't. But more importantly – and this is why I have dedicated a full chapter (Chapter 9) to personal branding – the main reason people didn't care was because they didn't know me as 'LIVinteriors'; they knew me as Liv Conlon.

It was my personal brand that was truly making the impact. When I received a recommendation via social media, clients never tagged my business; they tagged my name. People ultimately were buying from me. More on that later.

Your Brand Name

No matter what, I still believe that rebranding to ThePropertyStagers has been one of my best business decisions so far. Here's why:

- **It does what it says on the tin.** There is no mistaking that my team and I stage properties. There is no ambiguity; there are no 'interiors' in sight.

- **It positions us.** We are *The*PropertyStagers, positioning us as *the* ones to work with.

- **It's scalable,** both on an international scale and with my team. 'LIVinteriors' was centred around me as Liv; now that I have a team, the name encompasses all of us.

- **It's memorable.** Our brand stands out in all ways: it's bright, it's fun, it's easy to remember.

As we're on the subject, let's dive into naming your brand before we go any deeper into the principles of creating a household brand. As I've already demonstrated, the brand name that you choose today isn't the brand name that you are tied to forever, so let's not waste too much time over choosing it. The most successful brands I've created are the ones that I've spent the least time creating.

In my book *Too Big For Your Boots*, I discussed the Cup of Coffee method, which is: make yourself a cup of coffee (or tea) and by the time that drink is finished, you'll have chosen your brand name. Procrastination, which many people like to disguise as perfectionism, will be the killer of your business, so I'm challenging you. If you can't decide on a brand name in that time, I want you to choose the worst brand name that you can think of and this will be your beta name.

I'm taking this idea from *That Will Never Work*, the book by co-founder of Netflix Marc Randolph.[9] He origi-

---

9   Randolph, M *That Will Never Work: The birth of Netflix and the amazing life of an idea* (Endeavour, 2019)

nally called Netflix 'Kibble'; he knew the name was so bad that by the time he came to launch, he would be forced to change it.

Choose a name quickly. Don't let this be the thing that holds you back.

Tips for your brand name

Keep it simple. I always run any brand name past the 'phone call challenge'. If I speak to someone on the phone and they ask for my business name or email address, will I need to spend ten minutes spelling it out to them? Could they confuse it with something else? Keep your brand name short, simple and clean.

Do what it says on the tin. I would always suggest having exactly what you do stated in your brand name, for example 'Brown's Home Staging'. This will cut out any confusion over what service it is that you offer.

Check it's not common. First port of call when you have a name that you like is Google to check out all social-media platforms and domain names. Now beware: just because there is another brand with a similar name or the exact handle you want is taken, it doesn't mean that you cannot give your business this name. However, I would be careful that you aren't infringing copyright or trademark rights.

Secure the domains and social-media handles. When you find the one, secure your domain and social-media handles as quickly as possible. Make sure the domain has the correct country suffix (the .com part) and grab the closest social-media handle to your full brand name.

Conversation provoking, but not obscure. It's always a conversation starter if you choose a name that's a little different. Take my dog, for example. His name is Kevin and everyone asks why. Be noticeable, but don't make it too complicated.

Now that you've got your brand name, let's take a look at designing a brand look and feel that is aligned with your vision. You want to create something that doesn't already exist – why would someone work with you if there are ten other companies that are identical?

I'd like to introduce you to the brand sweet spot. It is the position in the market that nobody else operates in.

How To Find Your Brand Sweet Spot

Competitor research. Firstly, research which other home-staging brands are operating in your area at the moment. If there aren't many, expand the radius of your search.

My biggest tip here is to avoid going down a dangerous rabbit hole and comparing yourself to already-established businesses; this will only eat at your confidence and likely trigger imposter syndrome. You are taking a look at who else is out there for one reason and one reason only: to screenshot their logo and add it to a blank document.

Once you have completed your research, you will have a page that is filled with logos. This should make it easy to identify what stands out. You'll likely see a sea of similar colours and fonts and be able to pinpoint the exact brand colouring that rises above the others.

Inspiration. While competitor research will guide your brand look, ensure that it doesn't look identical to any other brand in the market. This is *your* brand to design as you wish; looking for what will inspire the look and feel is just a vital part to the process. My favourite way to find inspiration is by starting a new Pinterest board. I'll usually search for luxury brands or brands in my industry, finding colours and vibes that I want to embody.

All of this will help you create your brand look and feel. However, deciding your brand look isn't just the colours you choose, but every aspect that will contribute to your brand make-up. Various other elements such as typography, assets and signatures will build into your brand aesthetic across your social-media profiles, website, offline marketing and every touch-point with your client.

The feel. Remember back to Chapter 5 when you decided where you would like to position yourself in the market. Your brand feel has to encompass your price tag. It would feel as incorrect to have a low-end brand with a luxury feel as a high price tag with a student-vibe brand. Getting this right will determine who contacts you. Think, is your brand worthy of the ideal client you identified earlier?

Colour palette. Your colour palette will help you stand out visually from your competitors, so it is a great way to represent your brand feel. When I chose ThePropertyStagers' signature teal and pink, it stood out, but it also represented our company: fresh, bold and youthful. I suggest choosing a bold colour and a secondary colour that complements or contrasts with it.

Typography. Your brand should have three main fonts that you use throughout all of your assets and marketing. A title font (this is usually a similar font to your logo), a subheading and a body text. If you have a fancy logo font, I would suggest having two fonts that are clear and simple to read for your body text and subheading. I always think that if my brand logo was to be blown up to appear on a vehicle or billboard, would people be able to clearly read what it says?

Logo variation. If you have a certain shape of logo designed (ours is a rectangle), you will need to have variations of your logo created for profile images for each platform (circle and square). Consider using the initials of your brand name or your icon itself.

All of the elements of your brand will come together in a **brand-asset document**. This is your master document that will dictate any creative decisions. If you're creating content for your social-media profiles, designing your website or optimising your social-media pages, this document will include the logo, font, colour hex codes and guidance that you need so that at every touchpoint, you can ask, 'Am I on brand?'

To create your brand, you have two options:

1. **Do it yourself**. I would only suggest creating your brand yourself if you are a creative and are familiar with the technology you'll need to use. Also, you will need to be decisive and complete your branding in a timely manner. I personally love Canva, which has some fantastic templates, but beware. Many people use the exact same templates, and so you could end up having a very similar brand to someone else.

2. **Outsource**. You can outsource your logo and brand-asset creation via online sites. I personally recommend this option, as all you have to provide are your inspiration board and guidance and let the professionals take care of the rest.

Your Branding Everywhere

I believe that your brand extends from the minute you meet someone in person to how you present yourself online. It's in everything you do. It is crucially important to be on brand at every touchpoint with your client, especially as home staging is not a small-ticket service; it's a fairly large investment. Having a trustworthy professional presence is highly important.

Here, we will look at how to be on brand at every client touchpoint, both online and offline.

Online

Your branding online spans across your social-media profiles and your website. There must be a cohesive feel across all of the platforms – if I click on to your Facebook page, I should immediately recognise it as the same brand I see on your website.

Your website. You do not need a website to launch your business. I repeat: you do not *need* a website immediately. Many #StagerBoss students are successfully securing clients and building their brands solely through their social-media profiles.

While it's not a necessity to launch, a website is a necessity to scale longer term. It will give clients peace of mind that you have an established site and it will do a lot of your selling for you if you set it up correctly.

Ensuring that your website is fully functional across mobile and desktop is vital; a glitching or slow-loading website will immediately impact your clients' opinion of your brand and lose you business. If a site has poor performance, most visitors will leave.

Your social-media profiles. From your personal profiles to your business pages, there should be a seamless transition as your clients move from one to another. Each must embody professionalism. Your cover image, your profile picture, your bio and your content are representations of your brand.

If that means you have to do a clear-out of your pages, then start now. Any unprofessional images of a girls' night out or ranting posts that you've written in the past need to go. When you hold your brand-asset document next to each profile, the aesthetic of your pages should match, with a branded banner image and a professional profile image.

Your online profiles and website will be the first things someone will visit after meeting you in person. Is your in-person manner and professionalism continued on the screen? If their first impression of you is online before you meet or speak in person, will they be magnetised to connect with you or repelled? Your online presence is one of the most important elements to lead generation, so let's get it right.

Offline

While I am a big advocate of having a professional online presence, your offline presence is just as important. It's also lucrative. You may be surprised to hear that through our branding, ThePropertyStagers makes a considerable return on investment. Our branded vans alone bring in a considerable five-figure revenue per year. Never underestimate the power of people seeing you in the local area.

Let me share with you how powerful offline branding can be.

'Oh my goodness, Olivia, we have been following you on Facebook for years. We have been looking to buy on this street for the past twelve months and we saw your van. Is there a property for sale?'

I was staging a property in Glasgow, Scotland, and had ventured down to the van from the top-floor flat (for the twenty-eighth time that day). When a couple approached me and said these words to me, I quickly phoned my client and asked if they would agree to me showing the property, even though we hadn't finished staging yet. Luckily, I had my furniture team with me, so there was a total of three of us in the property; for safety reasons, I would never invite someone into the property if I was alone.

The result? Our client received an offer for the property within the first six hours of staging it. They didn't even have to list it with an agent and pay a large commission to sell it. The power of ThePropertyStagers' brand had created a buyer for them.

Think about the power of telling a story like this when a client is considering who to work with. Our branding sells! Here's another example.

'I've seen your van parked outside of the Dakota Hotel.'

Picture this: a fancy hotel and my van parked outside. Remember, I know my ideal client inside out and I know they have meetings in hotels like this (as do I). I had been parked for around an hour and I received a phone call from a man who had clocked ThePropertyStagers' van and was looking for our exact service. Forty-eight hours later and I was in his property with my team, staging it.

Never underestimate the power of having a presence in your local area. This is just one example of when our van has caught the attention of an ideal client; I've been called after being parked in a supermarket car park, on the main street in a small village, even stuck in traffic! And I've received enquiries from passers-by whose eye our branding has caught.

Let's look at the most powerful forms of offline branding:

- **Vehicle branding**. Branding your van or car (if you use it for work purposes) is a small investment upfront for a large return over the next few years. However, only brand your car if it is a vehicle that you're proud to be associated with your brand. For example, I am happy to brand my Mercedes vans, but I wouldn't have branded my ten-year-old car when I started out. You'll be looking to include:

  - **Clear logo and colours.** Think of this when designing your branding. ThePropertyStagers' teal and pink colour scheme is very striking.

  - **Brand motto/tagline.** While your brand name may do what it says on the tin, it's important to have a qualifying sentence / statement that encompasses what you do.

  - **Website**. Consider adding a QR code so people can simply scan it with their mobile.

  - **Contact details**. One simple call to action is needed. I suggest a landline number that potential clients can ring.

- **Clothing**. Everyone who works on ThePropertyStagers' team wears some form of branded clothing. This will vary dependent on season and the role of each team member. For example, our furniture team is equipped with t-shirts, sweatshirts and reflective jackets, whereas our staging team is equipped with t-shirts, sweatshirts, body warmers, baseball caps and woollen hats. Not only is this a marketing opportunity when the teams are out in public, but it also confirms in our clients' minds that we are a professional outfit.

- **Literature**. Consider business cards, brochures or fun swag that you can give to people at networking events or your own events. The main objective with this type of branding is to be able to tell your story and the importance of your service to your potential clients. Consider if you're working with a partner who will be recommending your service (eg an estate agent) providing a brochure that will sell what you do, rather than relying on the agent to fully explain the benefits of your service.

You've completed your masterclass on branding, but here's the thing: this is where I see most business owners stumble. Some will never launch or get a client as they are too invested in creating the 'perfect' brand. And I get it – I'm a recovering perfectionist. I want everything to be perfect, but to be frank, the perfect brand doesn't exist. I've had to learn the 80% cooked rule. If something is 80% perfect, I will publish it. I'd rather produce this than nothing.

Don't let the fact that you don't have branded vehicles, t-shirts or brochures stop you from launching. All you need to get started is your brand name and a beta logo; get clients first and you can work on the rest of it over time. Many #StagerBoss students get clients without a website or social-media page; don't let anything stop you!

Chapter Action List

This chapter has shown you how important your branding is to your success. It's time to move towards that success by taking action:

- Decide on your brand name.

- Create your brand inspiration board.

- Either create your own logo/brand-asset document or outsource.

- Implement your branding across your online platforms.

- Consider your offline branding (but don't let a lack of this stop you from launching).

9

Your Personal Brand
Is What Sells

Now that you know how to brand your business, let's talk about branding *you*. While it is vital to have a strong business brand, it is in effect just the professional authority that will elevate your personal brand. People won't buy from you because of your logo; they'll buy from you because of you. If you want to grow your business fast, which I'm assuming you do because you're here, you need to action a personal branding strategy.

Wondering how your business and personal brand fit together? Think of your business brand as your 'invoicing' brand. What does this mean?

- It's essential to have a business brand as it's the professional authority that sits behind your personal brand.

- People will make purchases from your business brand and be invoiced via your business brand, but they are really buying from you (especially if you run a small business).

- Your business brand will always be your secondary source of traffic, leads and focus. People will be more inclined to message you personally and buy from you via your personal profile, but they are purchasing your business's service.

Your personal brand is like pouring accelerant on to the growth of your business. What do I mean by this?

- Your audience will always connect more with a face than they will a logo, especially online. If a company contacts me, I'm much more likely to think it's spam than if a person contacts me.

- You (as a person) are more memorable than your business brand. There are thousands of business brands, but there is only one *you*. This is why I have no fear of anyone 'stealing' my business; I know those who connect with me will always work with me because of me.

- People will buy into *your story*. Nobody buys what you do; they buy *why* you do it.

- Your audience want to watch *you* develop on your journey. I have loyal followers who have watched my journey since day one, but only decided to work with me years down the line.

All you have to do if you want proof of the power of a personal brand is look at some of the top entrepreneurs in the world. While they have incredibly successful brands in their own right, if you see who gains more attention online (I'm using Instagram specifically as an example here), you'll find:

- Richard Branson has around 5 million followers; Virgin has around 300k.

- Mark Zuckerberg has around 11 million followers; Facebook has around 5 million.

- Russell Brunson has around 2 million followers; ClickFunnels has around 300k.

There is a reason that these entrepreneurs have more followers than their incredibly well-established brands. It's because we as clients want the human connection behind the company. They are the newsworthy leaders who we want more of an insight into.

This translates even more powerfully through to a small business (usually with a small marketing budget). My own personal brand has collectively around 30k followers across all of my platforms and ThePropertyStagers has around 10k. Whenever I am tagged online, even to this day, I am still tagged as Liv Conlon as I'm what people remember.

The Power Of Your Story

The question is, how do you build a successful personal brand? There is *one* reason that people will connect with you and that is. . . your story. Why is telling your story so powerful?

Your story actually changes the chemistry in your client's brain. It makes your audience feel more empathetic and connected to you, and this empathy is exactly what you need to convert clients. When you evoke emotion in your audience, you build (what I believe to be an overused but true saying) know, like and trust. Think about it. Have you ever bought from someone you don't like? I haven't.

If you want to be memorable, and I'm sure you do, tell stories. There is a famous maxim: "People remember stories 22 times better than facts alone." It's why this book is story heavy: I attach stories to my teachings so that you'll remember them when you implement the strategies.

Most people want to sell the benefits and features of their service, but that isn't what sells. Harvard Professor Gerald Zaltman carried out a study that showed "95% of our purchase decision making takes place in the subconscious mind",[10] meaning that once someone has emotionally bought into your product, they only need the features and benefits to confirm their buying decision.

This is why home staging works. When someone views a staged property, they fall in love with it. Only afterwards will they actually check if it has good storage and sufficient space for them to live in.

It is undisputed that telling your story is powerful and will speed up your success. However, it isn't always easy. Remember back to Chapter 3 where I shared how my fuel source was pain, especially in the early years of building my business. That wasn't comfortable for me to share, but I knew it was absolutely something I must do to create connection with you. In my first book, I couldn't bring myself to tell certain parts of my story and at every point in my journey, I've had to push out of my comfort zone to be able to share from an authentic place.

I have another story for you. Actually, I don't even know if I can take the credit for this as it was an accident when I unveiled my story of being bullied to a newspaper reporter who was interviewing me. I had been warned by my coach at the time that the columnist would be looking for something juicy, but

---

10   M Mahoney (2003) 'The subconscious mind of the consumer (and how to reach it)', Harvard Business School, https://hbswk.hbs.edu/item/the-subconscious-mind-of-the-consumer-and-how-to-reach-it

I thought that they'd be looking for some gossipy story, which I certainly didn't have. (I'm 24 and I go to bed at 8pm on a Saturday night.)

When I was concluding the interview, the reporter caught me off guard. They asked why I had left school at sixteen and my usual answer that I was a 'born entrepreneur' didn't quite cut it this time; the reporter must have picked up on the hesitancy in my voice. That's when I divulged that I hated school, the main reason being that I was bullied. I just couldn't keep it to myself any longer. I shared with the reporter my journey of being maliciously targeted by a group of girls, which resulted in me leaving that particular school and never returning.

Strangely, I thought I would feel a massive relief, but I didn't. What I did feel was shame. I had equated bullying with a lack in me: that people would think something was wrong with me, that I was weak. And so as the article 'Bullied schoolgirl to £1m business woman' was published, a little part of me died inside. I cringed at the thought of my old school peers reading it. I didn't want this title that I'd tried to hide for so long in the national news.

What I didn't know then was how it would change my life, and the lives of others. I had an influx of 2,000 followers and 562 Facebook message requests from women from every walk of life, age and background. Mums who had shown my success story to their kids going through the same trauma; women who were experiencing workplace bullying; women who no longer wanted to be on this earth. . . they felt heard. And for me, that changed everything. Originally a PR campaign to grow my business, this was now so much bigger. There was no turning back.

In being vulnerable in telling my story, I let go of who I thought I should be to become who I am. I realised that stories matter. If by sharing my experience, I helped one other person on the brink of suicide or giving up, it would be worth it. It was no longer about getting more Instagram followers to grow my business and reach; it was about building *connection*. In showing up vulnerably, I created a bond between myself and strangers.

I now love sharing my story to inspire and empower women. It's why I'm writing this book. You might feel like you want to do the exact same thing, but you might not be ready and that is OK. It took me over seven years to truly share every part of my story. I shared it only when I was ready.

Sharing my story enables me to connect deeply with people and carry out my mission, but I also want to highlight that it's an incredible business growth tool, too. Simply put, sharing my story helps my business. It may be hard to believe, but my team and I have people who stage with ThePropertyStagers over other home-staging companies because:

- They too were a young entrepreneur (even twenty to thirty years ago) and connect with me over that.

- They too have a family-run business, especially mum-and-daughter duos.

- They too were bullied when they were younger or a family member has been through something similar.

This is my story, so don't worry if none of the above has happened to you. You'll have parts of your story that I can't share as it's not my truth. One thing that's important to remember if you're wondering why people will care about your story: it's the *only* thing interesting about you. I hate to break it to you, but nobody is interested in your product or service; they want to know why it exists. And don't tell me you don't have a story. The fact you are reading this book tells me that you've got a memorable one.

How To Build Your Brand Story

How do you build out your brand story? Firstly, you identify your hooks. These are what make you interesting; they are the 'bones' of your brand story. You've just read some of my hooks: young entrepreneur; mother-and-daughter team; bullied in school. To identify your hooks, you need these four elements.

1. Your Origin A to B Transformation

Not to be confused with your client transformation statement that I shared with you in Chapter 7, this transformation statement is based on your origin story, which is why you started your business. Most businesses are born out of frustration; remember, we make decisions based on if they'll move us away from pain or towards pleasure. People won't care about any of the success you've had and they won't follow you or your advice until they know that you've been where they are now (you have likely at one point been your ideal client). When writing your brand story, you are inviting your audience along on your journey from where you started, showing them why you do what you do now.

Your Origin A to B Transformation comes in three parts:

- A = Where you started (likely where your client is now).

- S = Your solution (your product or service).

- B = Where you are now (where your ideal client wants to be after buying from you).

Example of an Origin A to B Transformation:

- A = My mum's property sat on the market empty for three months with no offers.

- S = I staged it.
- B = It sold within three days for £10,000 above valuation.

Tip: the secret is in the specifics. The more specific you are, the more trustworthy your story is.

2. Your obstacles and challenges

Often, what we want to hide is what we should shine the light on. Sharing the hardships throughout your journey makes you relatable; nobody connects with someone who is perfect.

With this hook, you want to highlight anything that came up on your journey of entrepreneurship or that inspired you to get started. For example, did anyone doubt you? I call this your underdog story proclaimed (USP), not to be confused with your unique selling point. Everyone wants to hear how the odds were *not* in your favour.

My obstacles and challenges:

- I was bullied at school.
- I was six-figures in debt before I started (not my debt, but still a challenge).
- I had to build my business with zero in the bank.

- The odds were stacked against me launching my business as a teenager with no industry or life experience.

3. Your previous experience and expertise

I always love when a #StagerBoss student tells me they have no experience to write about. If you're sixteen years old, like I was when I started in business, that is true; if you're older, you likely have experience to call upon.

Consider:

- Have you bought and sold or developed your own properties? Or assisted friends with theirs?

- Have you been involved in the property industry?

- If you have no experience in the property industry, what transferable skills from your last career can you bring into this new business? I like to put this into an X to Y statement; I've created some of the most weird and wonderful statements for my clients, but they work. For example:
  - From design engineer to designer of homes
  - From delivering babies to delivering staged homes

An example of my previous experience or expertise:

- My business stages over 400 properties per year.

- I'm a best-selling author.

- I've gone from staging properties to staging brands (and the reverse, as I'm now helping you).

4. Your achievements

Sharing your achievements creates an aspirational element to your brand. People like to follow and be associated with successful people, so:

- Have you won any awards?

- Have you been recognised in any publications?

- Can you state how many clients you've impacted or the collective value of the properties you've staged?

If you are starting out and haven't had any success yet, perhaps the fact you've left your nine to five to pursue a career you love is a win for you. You can also state who you are on a mission to impact over the next year.

An example of my achievements:

- I've won fourteen national and international business awards.

- ThePropertyStagers has been recognised five times as the nation's top furniture pack supplier and staging company.

- I've been featured in seventy-nine publications and featured on the BBC, ITV and more.

Your hooks will make up your brand story, also known as a bio. Your bio will appear everywhere: your social-media profiles and throughout your content. It is what someone would read if they were looking to interview you on a podcast or at a speaking event.

Your bio should include:

- Your name and the name of your business

- Your Origin A to B Transformation

- Your obstacles and challenges

- Your experience

- Your achievements

Here is an example of the bio that I used for my home-staging business. As you read, you will be able to identify the hooks that I've used throughout, even though they don't necessarily appear in the same order as they appear in this section:

> Many of the world's most successful
> business ideas are born out of frustration,
> and X-year-old Liv Conlon's million pound

business, ThePropertyStagers, is no exception. (**Name + business name.**)

When Liv's mother Ali struggled to sell her investment property after three months on the market, a then seventeen-year-old Liv had an epiphany: to stage the property. After staging, the property sold in three days for £10,000 above valuation. (**Origin A to B Transformation.**)

Currently operating throughout the UK, ThePropertyStagers and its team of ten furnish around 400 properties per year. What makes the business unique, aside from its exemplary reputation in the sector, is that its young founder has grown revenue from £30,000 in year one to £1 million in the space of twelve months. (**Expertise.**)

Tenacious and entrepreneurial to her core, Liv canned her early plans to go to university, instead leaving school aged sixteen without a business plan (**challenges and obstacles**), determining that she would be her own boss. Years earlier, aged thirteen, Liv had begun importing nail foils from China and reselling them via eBay at a profit. (**Experience.**)

It comes as little surprise, then, that today, this young businesswoman is fast accruing a mantle full of awards: fourteen in the past twelve months, including FSB UK Young Entrepreneur of the Year and the Legacy Education Alliance National Product. (**Achievements.**)

Having worked twelve-hour days for the past three years, laughing in the face of reverse ageism and delighting as Liv's mum Ali left her job to join the business, the mother-daughter duo are now reaping the rewards, with expansion from Glasgow to offering their service across the UK and an exciting partnership with some of the biggest property-training companies in the world. (**Challenges/ obstacles and achievement.**)

As you'll see, my bio covers all of my hooks and gives my audience an insight into who I am and what I've been through. I continually update my bio with a lot more of my recent accomplishments, successes and other businesses I have now founded, but I wanted to show you the version that was tailored specifically to my home-staging business.

Now that you know your hooks and how to write your brand story, there is nothing stopping you. Well, apart from one thing: *fear*! What most people fear more than anything is feeling embarrassed at starting small. You may be reading through my brand story and thinking that you don't have any of the things I've got.

Don't panic: before I started my bio, I had nothing to write in it; you'll likely have more than I did. But I did the most important thing: I started. It's taken me almost a decade to get to where I am today; there is no such thing as an overnight success. I'm not further ahead than you; I'm just on a different chapter of the book. With hard work and consistency over the years, you too can have a bio that reads like mine. But you'll have to go through the pain of starting small.

Confession time: sometimes I actually feel a little jealous of my clients who are starting out. They've got a completely blank canvas and can build their brand in the right way, rather than looking back with hindsight. There is no shame in being on an early chapter of your book. People want to see you develop on your journey; remember, some of my followers only bought from me after seven years. I'm not a believer in 'fake it till you make it'; however, I am a believer in 'face it till you make it'. You need to face the fact that you aren't quite there yet, but you will be.

Remember to visit StagerBossTheBook.com/bonus for your reverse engineer calculator, along with additional content and resources to support you on your home-staging journey.

Don't wait! The time to build your brand is now.

Chapter Action List

Now you understand how powerful your own personal brand is, let's get to work on creating it. You will need to:

- Decide on your brand hooks:
  - Your A to B transformation
  - Your challenges and obstacles
  - Your experience
  - Your achievements
- Write your brand story.
- Upload your brand story to your social-media platforms and website (if applicable).

10

Launch Your Brand
With A Bang

Firstly, congratulations that you've arrived at Chapter 10. I imagine you are as excited as you are anxious about launching your business and getting your first few clients. Don't worry, I've got you covered. I'm going to get you as prepared as possible to enable you to make the right kind of noise and, of course, attract your Paula.

Let's get planning the launch of your home-staging business. The launch phase is split into three different parts, but first, let's take a look at what you need in order to launch.

The secret to successfully launching your home-staging business as fast as possible is not to get stuck in analysis paralysis. Instead, take action; you possibly know by now these are my favourite words. What I often see is people wanting to have everything lined up and organised before they get out there, but if that's you, let me stop you right there.

You do not need to have everything in place inside your business to launch; otherwise, you'll likely never do it. Your goal is to get clients first; everything else is secondary. Furthermore, launching is where the real learning is.

Here is what you need to launch:

- Your signature service that you chose in Chapter 6.

- Your beta brand. Remember, don't spend too long on this.

- Your on-brand social-media profiles.

- A contract in place for when a client wants to go ahead. Please note, you cannot stage properties without a contract; you need to protect yourself, your business, your kit and your client. I give #StagerBoss students a copy of the contract we use inside our programme Staging Business Secrets.

That is *all* you need to launch.

You do not need a website or to own a kit, to have a warehouse or a van. You do not need to know the ins and outs of every single thing that it takes to run a home-staging business. This is analysis paralysis; you'll learn on the job.

I often see students procrastinating by putting five-year problems in front of themselves today. You are not at the stage of manufacturing your own furniture or hiring a team, not yet. You need a client. Just do it.

Pre-Launch

Your online presence is the easiest way to get as many eyeballs on your launch as possible. It's important to know that business is a numbers game: the more people that see your launch, the more successful it will be, so how do you achieve this?

'I felt like I was watching a teaser for a new movie coming out.' This is exactly how you want your audience to feel as you tempt them prior to your brand launch. It's how my audience felt before a new campaign I was launching at #StagerBoss called 'It's My Time to Shine'. The concept was to encourage women to claim their time to shine by ditching their day jobs and launching their businesses, but the pre-launch campaign was really what made it interesting.

I created a series of videos of me in a dark office (I had to wake up at 3am to film it; oh, and wake my mum up as she was the camera woman). There was a flashing and flickering light in the darkness. I was representing that women have been in the dark too long, not fully sharing their light. (If you want to catch the campaign, just head to my Instagram.)

Long story short, the campaign was incredibly successful. It spoke directly to #StagerBoss's ideal clients and created a *lot* of intrigue. The secret? The build-up.

I'm not saying these are the lengths that you must go to in order to launch your business (although, why not?). However, we can look at what made that campaign successful and break it down, so that when you come to launch your business, you avoid the mistake that I see almost every new business owner make: launching without a bang.

The benefit of launching is that you have the opportunity to make a splash as you enter the industry with a cool new brand that people have never seen before. Just posting one announcement isn't going to make any impact. This is what worked for my launch campaign:

- **Mystique.** I kept the message prior to the campaign brief and shared as few details as possible, apart from the date of announcement. No one had a clue what I was going to announce, but people were interested in what it would be. When there is mystique, there is intrigue, which grabs attention. Attention is one of the hardest things to catch.

- **Dramatisation**. I was in a dark room, reminiscent of a horror film. Who else on social media do you see doing this? It stopped people scrolling and added real drama to the announcement. It was Hollywood, hence why my client asked me if I was launching a movie. (That is on my vision board.)

- **A deadline.** I had a clear date of when the announcement would be coming. People had the date engrained in their brain by the end of the campaign.

- **Involvement**. One of the most fun and attention-grabbing parts was that I got many #StagerBoss students to send in videos of themselves saying, 'It's my time to shine.' When I collected all of these together, it made a really exciting video that generated a feeling of hype around the campaign. When people see other people involved, they feel fear of missing out (FOMO) and want to jump on to the bandwagon.

- **A period of build-up**. Most people will post the day before to say that an announcement is coming and there is no build-up of anticipation. If you do this, it is likely that most of your audience will miss that hint and will ultimately miss the big announcement. This is why I recommend you tease your announcement out over seven to ten days to create the biggest impact.

Your Contacts

You already have a network of people in your life: don't underestimate them. When you start a new business in the property industry, you'll likely be surprised:

- How many people in your life will be involved in the property industry in some capacity or another

- How many removed connections (acquaintances) could be great contacts

- How people will want to help you, if you ask for it

Tapping into these audiences is your quickest route to success. I call these people your warm audience, because you already have a connection with them and they will be the most receptive to your message. The best thing to do is to work out who you can contact. When you brainstorm this list, you may be surprised at how many people you actually know:

- Family

- Friends

- Service providers (your dentist, doctor, hairdresser – anyone who you have a relationship with)

- Any communities you are part of (church, sports clubs, parents at school, online communities)

- Previous colleagues or work-related acquaintances

- Friends of friends or acquaintances

- Social-media connections

Tapping into this warm pool will help build your confidence and your first client could definitely be someone you already know. I want you to push yourself outside of your comfort zone on this one. Speaking to people about your new business opportunity can be daunting, but you'll know from your own personal experience if it'll be easier speaking to your close family and friends or someone you know less well.

If you're feeling uncomfortable at the thought of sharing your business idea and in any way like it's a 'salesy' thing to do, I want to help you pivot your mindset on this. I'm a big believer that through selling, we are serving. When I'm speaking with my warm audience about a new business venture, I am not entering into the conversation thinking, 'How can I make a sale?' Instead, I ask myself, 'How can I add value for them?' Remember, your service can make someone a lot of money and in turn help support them in building their dream.

Another approach, if you don't feel like you could serve the person in front of you, is to ask for help.

Did you just seize up at the thought of asking another human being for help? I felt (and I am still working on it) the exact same thing and it's been one of my biggest areas of growth.

One of the scariest things I've ever done is when I asked Marc Randolph, the co-founder of Netflix, to write the foreword to my first book. I had invited him on to my podcast and managed to secure the interview (this alone shocked me). When I was speaking with my business coach Mike about my first book, he suggested that I needed to secure an inspiring entrepreneur for the foreword. I said to him that I couldn't think of anyone who would write it for me, then I told him that I was interviewing Marc the next day. He told me that I had to ask Marc. I knew he was right – when would I have this opportunity again? However, I really didn't want to; I felt sick at the thought.

As I sat in my living room, waiting for Marc to enter the Zoom room, my heart was pounding. I kept thinking, 'A girl from Glasgow on a podcast interview with one of the world's most successful entrepreneurs from Silicon Valley?' It was surreal. And made even scarier as I knew I was going to ask him a certain question at the end of the call.

As the podcast interview concluded, I asked Marc to stay behind for a few minutes, which he agreed to. I referred to what I was about to ask him as my 'Indian restaurant' moment. I had binged his audiobook of

That Will Never Work[11] earlier that morning, which took me nine hours, as I wanted to be as prepared as possible for his interview, and he had mentioned that one of the scariest moments of his career was when he took a potential investor to an Indian restaurant and asked him to invest in Netflix. This was exactly how this moment felt for me. With a shaky voice, I asked him to write the foreword, and he said yes!

When I ended the Zoom call, my mum was standing in the next room with her ear pinned against the door. She came in and we danced around the living room and celebrated; it was one of the best feelings in my life.

The moral of the story? Don't be afraid to ask for help. It's still to this day one of the most uncomfortable things for me to do; I am so independent. However, had I not asked Marc that day, I wouldn't have the co-founder of Netflix as the writer of the foreword to my book.

People want to help you. Whether it's your biggest idol or favourite celebrity, your mum or close friend, just ask them for help in growing your business.

When contacting your warm audience, you are going to approach this just like your online launch. You want to build intrigue around your new venture to capture

---

11 Randolph, M *That Will Never Work: The birth of Netflix and the amazing life of an idea* (Endeavour, 2019)

the attention and imagination of the person you'd like to connect with. I suggest that if you have a friendly relationship with this person, you secure an in-person meeting. This is the goal.

An invitation to an in-person meeting is where you create the intrigue. Instead of inviting someone by saying, 'Hey, I'm launching a home-staging business, can we meet up and chat about it?', say something more like, 'Hey, I've got something really exciting to share with you. Are you around on Wednesday? I'd love to take you for coffee/lunch.' By offering the person a free coffee or lunch, you are indicating that this is going to be an important meeting.

If you don't have a relationship with the person that's close enough for you to meet up with them, arranging a call with them will suffice. The key part of reaching out to your warm audience is that you do this in the pre-launch phase. Then they'll feel important because they're getting access to you and your exciting announcement before the rest of the world.

Launch Day

On launch day, it's full steam ahead. Let's get your brand launched!

If you've built anticipation in the run up to the launch date, then you should have a reasonable-sized audience who are excited and eager to hear the news. There are a few options when it comes to launching your brand; I suggest you implement as many as possible. This is the time to make the biggest splash when you have eyes on you, and won't it be worth it if you secure your Paula right out of the starting gate?

Let's have a look at your options in detail.

Video Announcement (preferably live)

The best way to deliver the news is via video. Why? Because people will connect with you more than a logo (hello, Chapter 9). Also, if you never put your face on camera, people won't know that this is an important announcement.

Your audience wants to see and feel your excitement as you explain the business, brand and services that you offer. If your video is live, you can flex your expertise by answering any questions that your viewers may have. Remember, most people's biggest fear is getting on camera. When I think back to my videos for my first three years online, they weren't the best; I looked like I was being held hostage in most of them! Just being yourself is your best strategy.

Social-Media Post

To continue the momentum, I recommend a direct announcement post on social media after you've posted a video announcement. This could be an image of your new logo, but I do advise that you are in the photo too (you'll receive ten times the engagement if you are). You could take a selfie with the logo displayed on your laptop or have it printed on to the wall behind you.

It's important that the caption explains the story of why you started the business, so mention your origin story and remember to let people know how you can help them. Insert a call to action at the end, advising that if anyone has any questions or would like to chat that they drop you a message online.

Brand-Launch Event

If you're really going all out, the best way to get attention is with an event. You can go big scale and invite the whole local community or you can just invite friends and family. Whatever you decide, this will create hype and FOMO for those who are not there, which will highlight that you are serious about your new business launch and people should take notice.

Sharing By Local Businesses

Your goal is to be exposed to as many people as possible during your launch and your ideal client may already be connected with a business in the local area.

Speak with any local businesses, especially property-related ones, and ask for a shout out on launch day. This could go a long way towards getting you noticed, but be sure to inform local businesses of how you too can add value to them in the future, whether that is a shout out for them or a partnership.

A Launch Offer

Want to make your launch extra special and entice your Paula to buy? Put together a launch offer that will be announced on the day. Position it as an early-adopter special.

If possible, don't discount your rate, but give potential clients a preferential deal – extra weeks on their kit rental, perhaps. Make sure that you put out a special word they have to quote when they want to work with you to receive the offer and a clear end date, eg valid for the next forty-eight hours only.

Post-Launch

Once you've launched your brand, it's important that you don't create hype, and then drop off the face of the earth. Eyes are on you now and potential clients want to get a taste of what your new company is all about. Build on the momentum that you've already created; disappearing is not the brand image that you want and people may wonder if you are even still around.

Here's how to continue your launch momentum:

- **Follow up with meetings or calls**. Get in touch with anyone who has expressed an interest in working with you or has asked for more information on your brand. When you're building relationships online, especially in the early days, it can be a good idea to take those relationships offline. Invite people to chat on the phone or for an in-person meeting.

- **Have content scheduled for a minimum of one month**. You want to be as prepared as possible, as I can promise you if you get a client during the launch phase of your business, all your focus will go to serve that client (as it should). You will likely abandon your online presence, so plan for this by scheduling all of your social-media content for your post-launch period and up to four weeks after. This ensures you don't disappear online and always have a consistent marketing message and presence. I'm going to talk all things online marketing in Chapter 12.

Now that you know how to gear up for a successful launch, let's get launching! Don't waste this opportunity. How good will it feel when your brand is out in the world and you find your Paula? In the next two chapters, we're going to discuss getting your very first clients.

Chapter Action List

Your launch is an exciting time. Here's how to ensure it all runs smoothly so you can enjoy this momentous occasion:

- Ensure you have completed the launch list:
    - You've chosen your signature service (see Chapter 6).
    - You've created your beta brand – remember, don't spend too long on this.
    - You've set up your on-brand social-media profiles.
    - You have a contract in place for when a client wants to go ahead.
- Plan seven to ten days of online pre-launch build-up.
- Plan your offline launch:
    - Write a list of your connections.
    - Reach out to your list.
- Plan and implement launch day, including:
    - Video announcement (preferably live)
    - Social-media post
    - Brand-launch event

- – Connection with local businesses

- – A launch offer

- Plan your post-launch:

    - – Follow up with meetings or calls.

    - – Schedule your one-month-in-advance of content (see Chapter 12 for more on online content).

11

Get Your First Paula Offline

'John from PPN in Edinburgh recommended you.'

If I'm being honest, I didn't even know who John was, but I was grateful to him when my new client booked me to stage his two-bedroom property and told me that I came highly recommended by John. I felt ecstatic; after attending seven networking events in the last few months with not a lot of business to show for it, I was finally starting to see the results of my efforts.

'It works,' I told myself. And so the next time a property networking event occurred, I decided to attend on the off chance that John would be there so I could give him a bottle of wine to say thank you for recommending me. As I entered the room, I scanned the faces to see if I spotted any familiar ones. I saw a man with a white moustache and hair (he was hard to miss) and remembered having spoken with him before.

As I approached him and caught a glimpse of his name tag, I was delighted to see that it said John. I went in with a friendly handshake, a big thank you and the bottle of wine. Luckily, he was the John who had recommended me (could it have been a more common name?). Our previous conversation came flooding back to me when I met him.

I had attended this same networking event eight weeks prior and I remember feeling a little deflated as I headed back on the one-hour drive to Glasgow. I'd spoken with many people, but felt like I hadn't got any good leads (you will sometimes attend events and feel exactly the same). No one had a property that they immediately needed to stage and I needed clients.

However, eight weeks later, I had a client as a direct result of attending that event. It was in this moment that I realised the power of networking and building my brand offline. John had no need for my service personally, but I had made an impact on him and I was memorable enough that when he was in conversation with someone who did need a stager, he recommended me. Like I said earlier, networking works.

Building a successful brand takes time. However, the work that you're doing now, especially with your offline marketing, is laying the foundations for your business the rest of the time. You never know who is watching when it comes to your online marketing, but with your offline marketing, you never know who someone else may know. Of course it takes time.

When you're building your brand offline, it is all about one-to-one selling (unless you're speaking from the stage), but it is a worthwhile investment, especially when you are starting out. Here are my recommended ways of building a name for yourself offline.

Networking Events

As I mentioned in the story above, networking events are a great way to meet your ideal clients. Where else would you find a group of them congregated in one room on a Tuesday night? However, being strategic with the events that you attend and in how you approach them is key to your success.

How To Attend The Right Events

Head to Google or a local event site like Eventbrite and search for 'property events'. It's as simple as that. Start by searching for those in close proximity to where you are based, and then expand your search.

Compile a Word document or spreadsheet of the events, tracking:

- The name of the event

- Link to book

- Date and location of the event

- Frequency (they are usually monthly)

- Audience size

- Name and details of the organiser (more on this later)

When researching events, you will be able to work out whether they are independently run or franchised. Both are beneficial; you will only be able to determine the quality of the event by attending.

How To Be As Prepared As Possible

There is nothing to stop you attending a networking event this evening; you literally don't need anything to attend and you'll find them educational and a great insight into your whole new world of property. I've heard many stories of #StagerBoss students backing out of attending events because they didn't have their business cards ready, but you don't need them. In fact, I'd prefer that you don't have them. If you don't have a business card and you meet a great connection, you can capture their contact details. Then you are in control of the follow up (the key to networking).

The fortune is in the follow up. I'll confess, I've attended networking events and not followed up with anyone I've met, but this is a waste of time. The gold is when you follow up with those that you've created a connection with and continue to be on their mind. I follow up with people, even if I don't feel there is incredible synergy between us to work together, and I ensure they have my contact details in case there is the possibility of a John scenario.

Be a good listener. In Dale Carnegie's book *How to Win Friends and Influence People*,[12] he teaches three rules to connect with someone: be a good listener, become genuinely interested in the other person and use their name often. 'A person's name is to that person the sweetest and most important sound in any language,' Carnegie states. I was shocked (and still am) when I attend events at how much people talk about themselves.

Do you feel worried about talking about home staging when you've not got a lot of experience? Don't worry: 80% of the conversation is going to be centred around the other person. It's funny – try it for yourself. And when you follow up, I guarantee they'll respond with how much they enjoyed talking with you (or rather, at you, lol).

---

12   Carnegie, D *How To Win Friends And Influence People* (Vermilion, 2006)

Join the Facebook group. Many networking events have a dedicated Facebook group and this is gold. Join the Facebook group for the event and add those as friends that you could see a potential synergy to do business together with; you now have an audience of your ideal clients in your area. You can also share value-driven content to the page to add value to the community and attract attention to your brand.

Speaking at events

The ultimate goal with every networking event that you attend is to become a speaker at the front of the room. When you present, you are instantly positioned as an expert and you go from one-to-one selling to one-to-many selling.

Imagine being able to speak directly to every single person in the room at once and only talk about your business and how much value you can add to the attendees. When I originally started out, I would attend networking events to grow my business; now I only attend them if given a speaking slot as I deploy a one-to-many strategy.

How do you get the opportunity to speak?

Connect with the host. The person in the room with the most influence is always the host. They are the puppet master and have the ability to get you on stage, but how do you get their attention?

- **Connect online**. When you purchase your ticket, the host of the event will likely be mentioned on the page. Search for them across Facebook, LinkedIn and Instagram, and connect.

- **Message pre-event online**. Message the host of the event to let them know how excited you are to attend. It is important that if you message them to say you'll be there that you do actually attend.

- **In-person connection**. When you arrive at the event, seek out the host. I recommend catching them early as many people will want to speak with them at the end.

- **Message post-event online**. This will be your third touchpoint with the host. Compliment them on the success of the event and ask for a speaking slot at one of their upcoming events. It's important here that you outline the value you'd like to add for their audience.

Preparing your talk. To keep yourself on track and enable you to visually engage with your audience, I suggest you have a prepared slide presentation with this structure:

- **Your story.** Yes, we're talking about your brand story again, which is why it is so key to become super clear on your hooks.

- **Why staging works.** Discuss the benefits of staging and include case studies and results from your own stages.

- **Your service.** You've explained who you are and added value through education; now is your time to ask your audience if it's OK with them if you explain a little about your service. Share with them the benefits of working with your company and what your service looks like.

Capitalising afterwards. The biggest mistake you could make is speaking at an event and not capitalising on it publicly. If there are only fifty or so people in the room, that is all you'll reach with your speech, but you can reach more. How?

- **Post an image online of yourself on stage (non-negotiable)**. You need an image of yourself on stage or, if there isn't a stage at the front of the room, a cleverly angled shot where viewers can see the audience. Ask your photographer to try to make the room look as full as possible. When your online following sees that you have been entrusted to speak in front of an audience, you will be positioned in their eyes as an expert as well.

- **Record your speech**. If you want to go all out, you could have your speech filmed or streamed live and uploaded to social media. Your talk could be watched by hundreds!

Attending an exhibition

Another great strategy to get face to face with potential clients is to rent a space at a property exhibition. Brand your stand to catch attention and be as engaging as possible; following the same principles we've just explored will guarantee you success. Tip: ensure there is a large footfall at the event so that you can receive a respectable return on your investment.

Hosting Your Own Event(s)

Now you know that the person with the most influence at a networking event is the host, it's time for you to become the host. When you are the host of your own show – which is not just limited to in-person events; it can also be a Facebook group if you are its owner and face, your YouTube channel or podcast – you can leverage this influence to scale your business. The leader of any group displays influence, especially in connecting with industry experts they wouldn't have access to otherwise.

I wouldn't have secured Marc Randolph to do the foreword to my first book if I didn't have a podcast. Inviting him on my podcast was a way to add value to him in return for his time. When you have your own show, very few people say no. However, I want to talk to you specifically about hosting your own in-person event.

Recurring Networking Event Or One-off Event?

Depending on your schedule and availability, consider whether your event will be a recurring event or a one-off. The benefit of running a recurring networking event is that you would continually be exposed to a returning and new audience. If you host these events monthly, you are reaching twelve times the number of people than you would hosting a one-off event.

If you host a one-off event, there is a lesser time commitment. These events can make a real statement, but they are also a lot of effort and energy for just one event.

My business's flagship event – one that I've hosted several times over the years – is called Breakfast with ThePropertyStagers and it has been a roaring success. Not only for the business's profile, but financially, too, with each event generating £20k+ in revenue and immeasurable revenue over time. I've met some of my best clients through hosting this event and they didn't even attend.

Let me share more on why this has been such a massive success.

A Unique Angle

Your audience is being bombarded with marketing each and every day, so you need to think how you are going to stand out. What is going to stop their scroll? Just like with your business launch, the secret to your success is creating intrigue by being mysterious.

With all things marketing, I like to add a unique angle. When I branded Breakfast with ThePropertyStagers, it was a play on the movie title *Breakfast at Tiffany's*; and yes, you guessed it: we offer a complimentary breakfast roll. Most networking events only serve tea and coffee, so this is another way to hook people in.

My team and I have hosted several Breakfast with ThePropertyStagers events, which take place around 10am. This may seem controversial to some, as you may think people who are employed are at work at this time, but we based this on our ideal client (think back to Chapter 7). Our ideal client isn't involved in property as a side hustle; this is their full-time career and as such, they are available throughout the day as they are self-employed.

I also hosted an Evening with ThePropertyStagers, a sister event that took place at night, but it wasn't as successful; the show-up rate was a lot lower than for breakfast. My analysis on evening events shows that people have unpredictable days and they can be steered off track. They may plan to attend, but other life things can pop up.

There Is Gold In People Who Don't Attend

Just because someone hasn't attended your event in person, it doesn't mean they can't be a lead. Actually, some of my key relationships have been with people I invited to an event, but they couldn't attend, and this is the gold in hosting your own event. Not only are you impacting those in the room, but also those not in the room.

When you're planning your event, employ a DM strategy to invite ideal clients. If someone responds that they can't attend, then meet with that person separately or jump on a call. One of the contacts I gained from doing this is the head of an estate agency in Glasgow; she referred two properties for me to stage before I had even hosted the event. Result!

You will notice a common theme throughout this book: and that is, you never know the impact you have made on the people you interact with and it's the same when you host your event. Just a few months before I wrote this book, a client booked ThePropertyStagers to stage his two-bedroom property; he had attended one of our events four years ago. With a combination of making a mark with your event alongside a consistent marketing strategy, you too can still be on people's mind in four years' time.

Key Partnerships

My final strategy to share with you to speed up the process to gaining your Paula is to build key partnerships. Right now in your business, if it's just you sharing your message, it will be an uphill battle if you have big vision and goals, which I'm sure you do. What if there was a way that you could multiply yourself? Building key partnerships, that can also be known as affiliates, will help you fast track your growth.

Who To Partner With

There are more people than you may think that you can partner with. Some of ThePropertyStagers' best referrers have been the most unlikely connections. The vital part to finding the right partner is to think who is connected to your ideal client already:

- **Estate agents**. A fairly obvious option is estate agents, who have access to homeowners selling properties every day. However, not every agent is going to get the vision of staging, or if they do get it, they may think that it's not necessary as 'homes sell in their area anyway'. Personally, I don't invest any time trying to build relationships with agents like this as I'm pushing against a closed door and my time is better spent elsewhere with agents who do get it. Enter with a mindset of abundance – plenty more fish in the sea. Only partner with agents who have the vision.

- **Letting or rental agent (long term or short term)**. If your signature service is the SA/HMO/student/rental furnishing side of the business (note to self: must find a way shorter name for that), the best connection for you is an agent that lets these properties; ideally one who is invested with the client from an early stage. For example, my biggest referrer in this part of my business is a short-term and holiday-let agent who sources, refurbishes and then rents the property for the client. They love working with ThePropertyStagers as we take the problem of furnishing the property off their hands and they know once they get the keys back, it will be ready to let immediately.

- **Your existing clients**. If you provide an incredible service and create raving fans, your clients will naturally recommend you to their network. However, if you find that one client is particularly active in the industry and is already a great source of business for you, setting up a more formal partnership arrangement can be beneficial for both parties.

- **Sponsorship**. You can sponsor a local networking event or charity gala that you know your ideal client will be part of. Invest wisely when looking at sponsorship; I'm always looking for some form of 'facetime' if I'm going to sponsor an event, meaning I will be given a speaking slot rather than a logo printed in a brochure that many won't even look at.

Referral Fees

Many of the people who recommend you will do it out of kindness. You've provided an incredible service and they're happy to share it with whoever asks. However, you may want to formalise and incentivise your affiliates to become more active in their marketing of your business.

This is what you need to know:

- **Don't offer until they ask**. I'm often asked by #StagerBoss students, 'What referral fee should I offer?' If your partners don't ask you for a fee, don't offer it. Many of my relationships are based on a mutual recommendation of services: if the partner recommends my business, my team and I will in turn recommend them (bear in mind that as home stagers, we make many people's jobs a lot easier). Think of it: if an agent is selling a property furnished versus unfurnished, it's an easier sale for them and the property is likely to receive a higher offer, resulting in a higher commission for them. If you are offering a referral fee, ensure that it is legal as in some professions, it is prohibited to accept a financial reward for a referral.

- **Treat your partners well**. If my team and I have conducted business with our partners, we ensure that they feel appreciated and valued. A little can go a long way. At Christmas, we will drop in wine for the office, or if there is a particular occasion where a partner has gone out of their way to help, we'll gift them with a bottle of champagne or a voucher. How you make people feel is the most important thing in business.

- **Set up a referral programme**. If you are excited about expanding your reach through the expansion of those recommending you, create a public marketing campaign and announce that you will be offering a referral programme. This can be a simple process, eg, when a client enquires about your service, they have an option to fill in a box to say who referred them. If and when that referral results in a stage, you can then gift the partner who recommended you their referral fee.

By now, you should be feeling confident in how to build your brand, starting locally and finding your first Paula. One-to-one selling is often the most effective strategy to deploy when you're starting your business as it gives you the opportunity to develop some strong relationships with those who already know you. However, it is also time-consuming and it may take you a long time to reach your goals, which is why your online marketing must be working in unison with your offline efforts.

Get ready for a masterclass on how to scale your brand online. That's what is coming in Chapter 12.

Chapter Action List

Offline marketing is hugely important to your business. This is especially so when you're first starting out, but don't forget the ongoing power of offline marketing as your business grows and expands.

Here's what you need to action to make a success of your offline marketing:

- Outline your local networking events:
    - The name of the event
    - Link to book
    - Date and location of the event
    - Frequency (they are usually monthly)
    - Audience size
    - Name and details of the organiser
    - Join the Facebook group for each event (if applicable)

- Connect with hosts of networking events / research exhibitions you could secure a speaking slot at

- Consider hosting your own event (longer term)

- Write a list of potential partnerships (estate agents, rental agents, existing clients, sponsorship opportunities) and reach out

12

Explode Your Brand On Social

It's no secret that I'm a big believer that the fastest way to grow your home-staging business is one-to-many selling online. I attribute my seven-figure success to my ability to harness the power of social media. As I shared with you in Chapter 7, it is how I've secured most of my biggest clients.

I want to take you back to my £260,000 client as there are some valuable lessons in this story that I haven't explored with you yet. I'm highlighting this story in particular as you are familiar with it. I have countless examples of other clients whose stories are almost identical; you begin to notice patterns when you've been in business for many years.

After this client's rejection of my first quote when he told me that I was too expensive, I felt down and, to be completely transparent with you, I was at a low point in my business. It was really tough and I toyed with the idea of giving up. I'm not trying to scare you, but I promised at the start of the book not to sugar coat the reality of running a business and I would be doing you a disservice not warning you that at times, you too will feel like giving up.

I wasn't seeing the results that I wanted and I questioned if I should do something else. Shiny-object syndrome kicked in – it does that, especially if you're feeling like something isn't working. But I decided to tough it out and keep going; I trusted in the process. Often, it's not the process that isn't right; it's the fact you haven't been doing it long enough.

I kept going, getting more consistent with my online marketing. I posted daily, showing up every single day, even when I didn't feel like it – and trust me, that was often. I got on live videos when I was in my warehouse, creating hype that didn't exist; I put my face on camera (with no make-up and looking exhausted) and gave tours of the properties I had just staged. It appeared I had little engagement; not many were liking or commenting, but I knew someone was reading, someone was watching. I just couldn't see them, until I received *that* DM:

'I've been following you online since we last spoke and I'm really impressed. I've just taken on a block of forty-five apartments in London, would you be able to provide a quote?'

Self-help author Napoleon Hill in his book *Think and Grow Rich* referred to being '3 feet from gold'.[13] This analogy comes from a story of a young man who was mining for gold for months during the gold rush. Then he decided to quit. He sold all of his equipment to a junk man, who sought advice prior to digging only to find out that there was gold just 3 feet from where the previous miner had stopped. The first miner was literally 3 feet away from striking gold before he quit.

I almost gave up not long before I got that DM from the game-changer client. The first miner – the quitter – could have been me, but what if this is you?

If I were to guarantee that I would transfer £260,000 into your bank account in twelve months' time, how would you show up? Would you show up daily, no matter how hard it was? Would you push through those moments where you feel like giving up? Would you put your face on social media even though it is kind of uncomfortable?

If your answer isn't a whole-hearted *yes*, that you would go all out, then turn back now. Don't embark on this journey. I can tell you now, the only way

---

13   Hill, N *Think and Grow Rich* (Vermilion, 2004)

you're going to be as successful as you wrote down in your vision is if you're willing to show up, no matter what, acting with the blind faith that the big payout or game-changer client is in your future. It could be tomorrow, in three weeks, nine months or two years from now; you will not be an overnight success. But I promise that it is coming if you write when no one is reading, create when no one is consuming and put in the work when no one is clapping.

Good, you're still here. I now know that you're willing to do whatever it takes, so welcome to your social-media masterclass.

A quick disclaimer before we dive in: social media is an ever-changing world with new trends, apps and features constantly being released. However, I want this book to stand the test of time, so I don't want to teach you about fading trends or pop-up platforms. The strategy that I'll be teaching you in this chapter is timeless as it focuses on connection. No matter what platform or form of media you apply this strategy to, the psychology of how you connect with people will never change.

What I love about social media is its accessibility: anyone anywhere in the world, if they have a device that can connect to the internet, can create a social-media account. We all start from the same position, with zero followers, and what a bonus: it's free! So the question is, if we all start from the same point, why are some more successful on social than others when it comes to growing their business?

Let's think of social media as a vehicle, say a car. We all have the exact same car and it will take us wherever we need to go, but we'll never reach our desired destination (the sale in this metaphor) until we add the fuel. If we insert the wrong fuel, the car won't move. If we insert the right fuel, the car will move.

Why do some people have success on social more quickly than others? They choose the right fuel, AKA the right strategy.

You can grow your business on social media:

- No matter what age you are

- Whether you are tech savvy or not

- No matter how many followers you already have (I generate seven figures with under 3,000 followers)

- Without any ad spend

In essence, all you need is the right strategy. I'm going to share with you the *exact* strategy I applied to social media to create a seven-figure business in under two years and, remember, with only a few thousand followers and no ad spend. It's important to point out that I'm not special; my students are implementing this exact system and creating massive success too. Are you ready to follow in their footsteps?

Most people when they hear the words 'social media' seize up, but I don't want you to feel this way. Social media is a simple concept. Let's break it down:

Social	Media
Relationships	Content

We create relationships online via the content that we share, simple! Often, the part we forget about social media is that it's all about people: there are humans behind the screens. Do you have relationships in real life? The answer, of course, is yes, so you're capable of building them online.

Let's start with people. When people visit your profile and website online, this is known as traffic. I like the idea of thinking of my audience as traffic because this isn't something I create; it already exists. All I have to do is stand in front of it (metaphorically). This changed my perspective as I didn't feel under so much pressure as my audience is already out there; I just needed to be able to catch their attention.

But first, we must all ensure we're searching in the right places, AKA platforms. If we are active on the right platforms, it's like being on a busy road at rush hour. There's traffic everywhere. If we're on the wrong platforms, it's like being in the middle of the desert.

Which platforms are the most powerful? I suggest being active on three platforms: Facebook, LinkedIn and Instagram. Let's break it down.

Facebook

Facebook is one of my favourite platforms as it has been the most powerful for me to build my profile and become recognised in the industry (I've got the blue tick now that certifies my account as verified). The property community is very active on this platform, so integrating into their already-formed groups is key.

Facebook was *the* platform that enabled me to scale my business to seven figures. I identified that my dream client spends a large majority of their time on Facebook groups, engaging with their tribe. As you know, I started my business with no funding and have taken no investment since day one, so mastering organic reach and cultivating relationships within these property communities was key.

Join Existing Communities

The Facebook group feature helps you to easily connect with existing communities in a similar way to attending networking events. This is perfect: where else will you find an already-formed community of your ideal clients? And this tribe don't only congregate once a month.

However, joining a Facebook group is not a sales opportunity; it's a nurturing opportunity. Selling to a Facebook group is the quickest way to receive an eviction notice. All of your content has to be value driven with the view to serve.

Create Your Own Facebook Group

Become the host of your own show. This way, you call the shots and influence your community, but beware. Hosting, running and maintaining engagement in a Facebook group is no small feat; it's a long-term commitment, but the benefits can be huge.

Build Your Business Profile Through Your Personal Profile

As you already know, personal branding is everything and this is no different when it comes to your online profiles. Building client engagement through your personal profile is incredibly powerful and puts you in control of growing your audience. By using the friend-request button, you can add people who you would like to see your content but please do not send out numerous requests at once. Of course, they have to accept, but this is a way to grow an audience more quickly than via your Facebook business page, where you have to hope that the right people will like it.

I post all of my content on to both my business page and personal profile, but my business page is my secondary source of traffic. Facebook will limit the reach of my content there because I'm not paying for it.

If there's gold in Facebook groups, how do you ensure you're in the right place?

Identifying The Right Groups

By host. The best place to start searching for the most connected Facebook groups is by searching by host. The goal is to be in the most active communities with the most influential hosts. Here is how I search for them:

- Research and identify the influential figures in your industry.

- Search for those people on Facebook. If they have a community, it will appear on their profile.

- Request to join.

By location. The next best way to search for the most active communities is by location. Head to the search bar, type in property and filter the result to group and location. If you can't find groups locally, expand your search to the nearest town or city.

By programme. Property-training programmes have some of the most powerful Facebook groups that I've ever been part of. They are usually groups connected to all the people who have purchased the online or in-person programme. The only issue with this is that you need to be a student of the course, but it could be worth it to create some powerful connections.

By networking events. If you're attending networking events, always ask the organiser if there is a related Facebook group. This is a strong fusion of online and in-person connection.

Infiltrating A Facebook Group

It's not as shady as it sounds, but this isn't an overnight strategy (you may realise I say that often). Brands have spent years building a niche community of highly engaged people, so be wary of being the new kid on the block. You need to work your way in slowly, providing high value to the members, which will ultimately result in you being seen as the go-to expert in this space.

Be sociable and help. The easiest way to build a household name is to add value and *help* the community you are serving. That means when group members are asking for advice, you are replying to their comments. I will commit twenty minutes per day to logging into Facebook groups, offering help, support and feedback even if it is unrelated to staging.

Post original educational content. Never, I repeat, *never* promote yourself or your services directly into a group. Most likely, an administrator will give you a strong warning or you'll be removed, plus members will begin to dislike you. However, there are indirect ways to demonstrate your services without selling, such as sharing a before-and-after transformation of a property, explaining the different design elements that your dream client could implement for themselves.

Instagram

I encourage you to build your presence on Instagram, but all too often, I see home stagers focusing way too much of their time on this platform. While it is the most enticing social-media platform with its media-driven content, it's also the platform you have the least control over scaling. With both Facebook and LinkedIn, you have the power to add connections; with Instagram, you are hoping that someone follows you.

From my own data, only 10% of ThePropertyStagers' social-media enquiries come from Instagram, and so I focus my team and my own time on the platforms that truly deliver. With that said, here are the elements to Instagram that I love.

The Perfect Mini Portfolio

Don't have a portfolio yet? Instagram will serve as your mini home-staging portfolio when you're starting out.

Instead of going to the effort of creating your website, when you're starting out, you need to focus on securing clients. If a client asks to see your work, send them to your Instagram profile where you can give them a taste of what your style truly is. It doesn't even have to be your own images; you can use images from the web that have inspired you, mood boards and images of yourself. The client's initial reaction will be to look at your grid (the collection of visuals you share with your followers) overall instead of clicking into each individual photo. If you are using any images that aren't yours, it is vital to request permission from the owner of the image and always credit them in the caption.

Create FOMO

Whoever thought content that disappears after twenty-four hours would work? But it's actually one of the most successful features to be created on social media. It engenders FOMO in your audience as there is the disappearing element to the content that you produce on Instagram.

More and more, our audiences are craving the realness behind our brand, and as Instagram stories are uploaded in the moment, they tend not to be as staged as feed posts. Russell Brunson suggests that Instagram stories are like having your own reality TV programme.[14]

---

14 Brunson, R, *Traffic Secrets: The underground playbook for filling your websites and funnels with your dream customers* (Hay House, 2020)

The Hub Of Collaboration

Instagram is the hub of collaboration as it is the perfect location to do a shared reveal of your most recently staged properties with any key partners. All of you will receive the engagement and it makes a clear statement that you are partnering with others in the property industry.

One of my favourite things about this platform is the large selection of media that you can utilise to engage with your dream client and community. It's also optimised for visuals, which is perfect for all things home staging.

LinkedIn

LinkedIn is my second favourite social platform, after Facebook. The difference between Facebook and LinkedIn is the intent behind the users.

On Facebook, users are scrollers; they are not nec-essarily looking to buy something and they use the platform in their spare time. LinkedIn has a more focused business intent: people are on this platform to get or give business.

Picture it like this: people are on LinkedIn while in work mode and on Facebook at the weekends. Where Facebook comes into its own is the community element, which LinkedIn doesn't excel in. These are my own personal insights from my experience.

LinkedIn is a powerful platform because users are business focused and as such are likely to do business, or at least have a conversation about it. Looking to attract dream clients? You want to speak to decision makers. There are literally hundreds of millions of decision makers on LinkedIn. Do you think you could find your ideal client among them?

Like Facebook, LinkedIn puts you in control of growing your audience. By using the add connection button, you can choose who you would like to see your content. The reach of your LinkedIn business page, while I always encourage you to create one, will be much poorer than that of your personal profile. It's always the way.

The Secret To Leverage LinkedIn

This feature of LinkedIn blows my mind every time I use it: the search bar. You can literally search for your dream client in the LinkedIn search bar. Type in their job title and location and you'll find hundreds if not thousands of results.

Better yet, if you're really serious about scaling on social, sign up to Sales Navigator. This is quite costly, but worth the investment as you'll be able to get even more granular with your search results and reach out to those you aren't even connected with.

It is a different audience on LinkedIn compared to other social-media platforms. They are not as concerned about the aesthetic as those looking at a curated Instagram grid, for example. In my decade in the industry, through trial and error, learning and tracking my business's results, I've found these are the most successful ways for a home stager to post on LinkedIn:

- **Long-form caption posts**. LinkedIn is a great place to start a conversation, especially an intellectual one. Your audience wants to be able to engage, give their opinion and discuss the content you are posting. This is one of my favourite places to discuss the high offer ThePropertyStagers' clients receive after staging their property, myth bust different opinions people have of home staging and even challenge my audience on some of the reasons people don't stage their property. In summary, don't be afraid to get controversial and polarising, but be ready for the heat if you do.

- **Articles**. If you are blogging on your website, LinkedIn Articles is the perfect place to repurpose that content. If you are new to the blogging world, the article section on LinkedIn is a great way to assert authority and position yourself and your brand. Offer unique perspectives and don't be afraid to polarise your audience.

- **Video walkthroughs**. Photographs can do your staging justice, but videos of the property really bring it to life. Whenever you're creating content, always think 'repurpose'. My team and I post every property that we stage to Facebook Live and repurpose the video on to LinkedIn with a caption explaining the layout of the property. Even better, tag your client. They are then likely to share with their audience, which works as social proof for you and will get hundreds of new sets of eyes on your brand.

Apply The Strategy

Now that you know where to find your ideal client, you need to create content to get their attention and create connection with them. You may have noticed, I'm a data-driven person, and to scale my business, I created a strategy that I could follow myself and remove the guesswork around what content was converting my audience and what wasn't. For the past decade, I have tracked my top-performing content and placed it into a method that all of my most successful students are implementing. I implement it personally to this day to generate seven figures in revenue each year.

I share my full ten-part Home Staging Content Strategy in the #StagerBoss signature programme, Staging Business Secrets. If I were to break down all of these ten content pieces, I could have a 100-page book on this subject alone. However, I want you to have everything you need to launch, so I'll dive deep on two pieces of content you can write.

HOME STAGING CONTENT STRATEGY

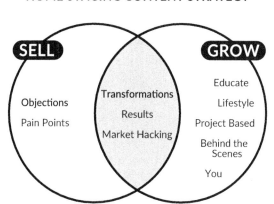

You'll see that the content strategy is split into two sections. This is because there can only be two purposes behind your content:

- **To sell.** This is the content that sells your services. If you only nurtured and never threw out any calls to action, then your audience would never convert. Your audience is looking to you to tell them what to do. They also want it made very clear how they can buy from you – remember, it's a disservice not to tell them this.

- **To grow.** This content will grow your audience, reach, influence, reputation and trust. If you were to try to sell to and convert your client in every piece of content that you create, your audience wouldn't be around long. Nurturing your audience is the key to converting them over time.

I like to think that this content to grow my audience indirectly sells my business's service as it's building the trust and one day, the client will purchase. My team and I build connection with our audience through sharing our story (and our personal brand) or giving them tangible value and education so that they leave asking, 'If this is what they give away for free, what will I get if I pay them?'

In the overlap of the circles in the diagram, you'll see some content that actually grows your brand *and* sells at the same time. Let's look at two content pieces to help you grow your audience and sell your service.

You Content (Grow Content)

Remember your brand story? This is how you communicate it less formally throughout your content. This type of content puts a bow on who you are, your unique brilliance (there is only one you and that's why people will buy from you).

While this isn't strictly business related, it is the content that will receive the most engagement. People will emotionally connect with you via this content, which as you know, indirectly sells you as you're building know, like and trust. This content is where you share the things that you want to hide, as these are often the things you need to shine a light on. It is about growth as it will not only attract a new audience, it will continue to nurture and grow your connection with your existing audience.

Here is an example of you content. This was accompanied by an image of me at a conference wearing a bright dress and cowboy boots before I spoke on stage:

Cowboy boots and an audience of 500 at the International Home Staging Conference.

Feeling reflective:

Starting @the.propertystagers at my desk in my bedroom at sixteen.

Scaling a seven-figure business by nineteen.

Speaking on an international stage in the USA at twenty-one.

Not a bad Friday – let's see what happens next. But first, a weekend in the home of country music.

Let's break it down. I'm showing some of my personality and an insight into me with the mention of cowboy boots and that I love country music. I'm not bragging that I'm speaking at this conference as I'm sharing my underdog story: the fact that it looked unlikely I'd be here at twenty-one from starting my business at sixteen. I'm positioning myself as the expert in my space as I've been invited to speak on stage on another continent, but I'm humbly highlighting my achievement.

Objections Content (Sell Content)

How do you like the idea of turning a negative objection into a positive that will bring you lots of clients? Yes, I'd take that!

This content is all about taking inspiration from your conversations with clients. Why have they said no to working with you? You want to document each objection as I guarantee if one person has been thinking it, many more will in the future. If you can say it to them before the client voices their objection out loud and justify an answer, you'll eradicate any doubt they have about working with you as they'll believe you can truly get in their head.

Here is an example of objection content:

'I can do it myself.'

Absolutely take on the challenge of furnishing your property yourself, if you dare. Order furniture online and schedule it all to come at once; wait on furniture arriving at sporadic times; remove and dispose of the packaging; shop at multiple shops for everything you need and return to those shops 100 times because you never actually know how much stuff you will really need; have the right tools for building furniture and hanging canvases; carry bags of accessories, such as ironed bedding, up dozens of stairs; build the furniture; hang the artwork; position accessories. Do all this while being a full-time designer, and then take the marketing photos. Oh, and if you're selling your property, dissemble and remove everything you have just installed when the sale has gone through and store it somewhere.

Don't worry, lots of ThePropertyStagers' clients have thought the same, done it themselves and come to us to stage the next one. Don't be that person. By the time you calculate how long it will take to do all of that, ThePropertyStagers' team could be finished.

Oooh, burn!

Let's break this objection content down. Start the piece of content by quoting exactly what the client is likely to say and is currently thinking. This is going to grab their attention and they will instantly want to click to read more.

Then outline everything they haven't thought of yet, all of the work that really goes into staging a property. This will shock them.

I had a little aha moment the other day. I've designed custom-made sofas and I'm manufacturing them for my house in Spain, but when I received the quote to get them shipped over, I immediately thought it was too expensive. Then I calculated how much it would cost in both time and money to do it myself and it was actually cheaper to go with the company.

Your client will have objections that they have not fully thought through. This is not about shaming your client; it is key that they know they're not the only one to have come up with the objection, hence why you let them know others have thought the same too. In my example, I'm being quite controversial as I'm overtly confident in ThePropertyStagers' service and challenging the client not to be like other people and make the same mistake. This will feed into their competitiveness.

Implementing just two of the ten pieces of my content strategy will differentiate your content from everyone else's in the home-staging industry. However, I want to leave you with one final formula that will bring this chapter and your online marketing strategy full circle. You can use this formula to audit your social-media growth. If you aren't converting your audience, I can guarantee you are missing one of the three elements of the Success Formula:

The Success Formula
= (Value + Consistency) × Share

You need all three elements of the formula to be successful:

- **Value:** you add value to your audience and fulfil a need.

- **Consistency:** you show up daily online.

- **Share:** do you actually publish or are you a best-kept secret?

The perfect scenario is that you write consistently high-value content that connects with your audience and you post it daily across all platforms. This is why you are converting clients on social. If the perfect scenario is not your reality, then you are missing at least one of the elements of success. Let's break it down.

Scenario # 1: Value is missing:

$$(\underline{\quad\quad} + Consistency) \times Share$$

You consistently publish, you are making noise, but not the right kind. Your content is low quality: it offers no value to your audience and it doesn't connect.

Scenario # 2: Consistency is missing:

$$(Value + \underline{\quad\quad\quad}) \times Share$$

Your content is on point and what you write, you publish, but you only publish a few times a month, so you have not built momentum and are not seen as the go-to expert. In other words, people don't know who you are.

Scenario #3: Share is missing:

(Value + Consistency) × ____

You create a high quality of content that follows the strategy and you write it consistently, but you never actually post it. It sits in a document on your laptop and you never reveal it to the world, so nobody knows you exist.

You need to embody all three elements of the Success Formula to convert your audience. As I've said many times throughout this chapter, success will not come to you overnight, but you've got to start somewhere. It's important that you continue to write when no one is reading, create when no one is consuming and put in the work when no one is clapping. Your day is coming!

Chapter Action List

Your online presence won't reach all your ideal clients overnight; it's an ongoing process which relies on you showing up consistently with high-value content, come what may. In this chapter, we've looked at the ways you can do just this, including:

- Write a statement of committing – how will you show up every day?

- Set up your profiles on Facebook, Instagram and LinkedIn.

- Brainstorm five ideas for 'You' and 'Objection' content.

- Write ten captions in total and schedule these on social media.

13

Your Next Level Awaits

It's true, you do want more. I've warned you many times throughout this book that it's not an easy path you've chosen, but the fact that you're still here shows your commitment to this journey. However, this is just the first step.

It can feel like an accomplishment in itself, finishing a book, and it is, but when it's a book that is calling you to action, the differentiator is if you take that action or not. You've read a book, but you don't actually know how to launch a home-staging business until you do it.

The Principles To Embody

In this final chapter, I want to help you be the one who does take action; the one who beats the odds and launches a stand-out home-staging business. There are a few principles you need to embody.

Become Obsessed

I love it when I speak with a #StagerBoss student and they tell me that they are willing to do whatever it takes to be successful in building their business. I will then advise them that they need to record a video of themselves talking about their business and all of a sudden, they're willing to do everything except for a list of the five things that make them feel uncomfortable.

If you truly want this – if you want the vision that you set out for yourself in Chapter 4 – you'll do anything to make this work, no matter how uncomfortable you feel. I know this because it's the same level of commitment that took me to where I am today and the students that I see excel also do whatever it takes.

Prioritise growing your business over everything else, and your life will become unrecognisable in the next twelve months. Don't kid yourself, though; if you're not willing to do the things that cause discomfort now, don't embark on this journey.

Become A High-Quality, High-Output Individual

If you can create in a week what it takes other people a year to do, you will be the most successful person in your industry. Money follows speed. Industry leaders have a higher output than their counterparts. They produce more content and ideas, and they are quicker to market with them than anyone else. They understand that time is of the essence, but they only focus on 'needle-moving' projects for their brand, ie, tasks that move their business forward.

My favourite method to become a high-output individual is 'deep work'. This term was created by best-selling author Cal Newport and he explains it perfectly in his book of the same name.[15] In the book, he refers to his concept of deep work as 'professional activities performed in a state of distraction-free concentration that push your cognitive capabilities to their limit. These efforts create new value, improve your skill and are hard to replicate.'

In studying the lives of the most successful entrepreneurs from both distant and more recent history, he found that deep work is a common theme. To succeed at constantly innovating, you have to produce the best stuff you are capable of and these tasks require depth. Most entrepreneurs will not be successful as they aren't willing to commit to the method of deep work.

---

15   Newport, C *Deep Work: Rules for focused success in a distracted world* (Piatkus, 2016)

In prioritising this in your life, not only will you be able to achieve your vision, but also a more balanced life, which I believe to be crucial to your success. See deep work not as deducting time from your life, but giving it back to you. This is as opposed to operating from shallow work, which is full of distraction.

I'm often asked by students if deep work can be bypassed as we all have busy lives, but my opinion is that it absolutely cannot. Although it may appear a burden, in deep work, you create an elite level of work. You will not become successful without practising it as you will not possess the concentration level required to tap into your genius.

Stay In Your Lane

There are going to be an unbelievable amount of distractions along your journey. There will be shinier, sexier business opportunities that pop up and other services that seem like they could make you money quicker. But here's the thing: I advise against having multiple focuses not because I'm the killer of fun, but because I've experienced first-hand the pain that will occur when you veer off course.

You'll never be successful at anything unless it is your sole focus. In Russell Brunson's book *Dotcom Secrets*,[16]

---

16 Brunson, R *Dotcom Secrets: The underground playbook for growing your company online with sales funnels* (Hay House, 2022)

he suggests that you build one funnel and don't build another one until that original funnel has hit $1m in revenue. I carry that same principle through to my #StagerBoss students. Don't get distracted; niche down to one specific service and stick with it. You'll never reach your goals unless you do.

Put The Blinkers On

One of the biggest things that will hold you back on this journey is getting caught up in what other people are doing. I have a no-show policy in my company, which means that I don't want to be shown what a competitor is doing, *ever*. My team only watches to see if something breaches my trademark or copyright, which would result in legal action.

I block people on social media who negatively impact my mental health. I know looking at what others are doing will only make me feel insecure or uncertain in my own path and as the leader in my business, I have to have crystal-clear vision. I love this statement from Dan Kennedy, the grandfather of marketing:

'I look at what everyone else is doing – and I do the complete opposite.'[17]

This is exactly the motto my team and I live by. Hence, you don't see us doing things the normal way.

---

17 Kennedy, DS *No BS Marketing to the Affluent: No holds barred, take no prisoners guide to getting really rich* (3rd Edition, Gildan Media, 2019)

Refresh Your Vision And Concretise Your Income Goal

Just because you've created your vision board and written down your monthly survival budget once doesn't mean you can forget about it. You should be looking at your vision and goals daily (display them somewhere in your home or office that you see every day).

I like to revisit my goals and vision quarterly to assess if a course correction or realignment is necessary. My process for this is what I call a 'one-person mastermind'. I will deliberately schedule a few days in my calendar every quarter to take time out and assess where my business is and where it wants to go.

The secret to success with this is that I never do this in my own home or office (wherever I spend most of my time) as it limits creativity and it can hinder expansive thinking. Instead, I book somewhere that will inspire me, usually a five-star hotel, for a few nights. Taking this deliberate time out in an elevated environment gives me complete silence to really map out my next moves.

Take All-Out Massive Action Now

The best time to plant a tree was twenty years ago; the second best time is today. Don't get upset about the action you haven't taken up until this point in your life, but do not waste another day.

To be frank, there is never going to be a perfect time in your life to launch a business, because life is always busy. There will always be a reason that you should delay this until next week or next month, which will quickly turn into a year and nothing has changed. Those who take action quickly will be the most successful, so don't let this book be one that you read and forget about. I am handing you the roadmap to launch a business that will change your life, but it's your responsibility to take action. Don't overthink this; follow and implement the action list.

Commit To One Path of Learning

I'm often asked by my students in #StagerBoss's signature programme Staging Business Secrets, 'Liv, what books should I be reading?' I will always answer this question with a question:

'Have you completed all of the Staging Business Secrets curriculum and consistently implemented every action point?' If the answer is no, which it always is, then they shouldn't be looking at any other books, programmes or courses.

Staying on one path of learning is crucial, otherwise you'll enter into analysis paralysis and learn strategies, methods and systems that are completely unrelated to growing a home-staging business. It's another form of shiny-object syndrome. Everything you need is at your fingertips – it's in these pages and through the resources that #StagerBoss has to offer. I created everything I teach as I wanted to condense my decade of learning into months for you. I only wish I'd had this book when I was growing my business.

Join Staging Business Secrets

In this book, I've left no stone unturned. If all you do is take the strategies and methods that I've taught in these pages alone and implement them with all-out massive action, you will launch a successful home-staging business. But if you are like me, you want success today, not in six months, not in twelve months.

I'm always looking at how to shortcut my success. It's why I've spent over £250,000 on courses and master-minds over the last decade. I value my time and know that investing in programmes with the person who has already achieved what I want to achieve will fast track my success. They have condensed their decades of learning into months for me and now, I now hold the map.

If you are like me and you're feeling called after reading this book, I would like to personally invite you to join me in fast tracking your success in Staging Business Secrets. Staging Business Secrets will:

- Hand you the exact directions and map for how to get to your goals as quickly as possible. You'd never drive to a destination you've never been to before without a map, so why not take the easy route and tap into mine?

- Hold you accountable through group sessions to stay on track of your goals. We all know life can get in the way and we need a course correction sometimes.

- Give you every tool, document and resource you will ever need (including the contract that I give to my clients) to ensure you are running a professional home-staging business.

- Offer high-level mentorship and accountability. Proximity is power and in Staging Business Secrets, you are going to have proximity to me and those who are already running wildly successful home-staging businesses.

- Connect you with a community of women who are on the same journey as you. This tribe of women will be a source of inspiration and support; many #StagerBoss members have become lifelong friends.

If you truly want this – and what you've learned in this book has been enough to show you what's possible – then why not ensure your success and give yourself every opportunity to make it happen? Staging Business Secrets is #StagerBoss's industry-disrupting signature programme, one of the only programmes globally to teach on both staging-for-sale and staging-for-let services.

My team and I have been playing in this market assertively since 2016 and have a wealth of real-world knowledge, experience and a proven track record of results. What makes our programme different to anything else in the market is that we run a successful home-staging company first and an educational company second, which gives us the best opportunity to provide the highest level of real-time education to our students.

Think of Staging Business Secrets' elite, proven blueprint as a download from my brain on how to holistically launch and grow your home-staging business. In our all-encompassing programme, you'll learn not only how to launch your business from zero, attract dream clients through innovative marketing strategies and scale your revenue, but also how to implement the systems and build the team you need to support the life of your dreams. With the help of mentoring, accountability calls and your new tribe of women, you'll become an unstoppable force in your industry. Whether you want to go full time in the fastest time possible, create a six-figure income or even supplement your existing income in your current career, Staging Business Secrets will walk you through it.

If you're serious about building a successful home-staging business, then give yourself this gift and opportunity. To find out more and join Staging Business Secrets, visit StagingBusinessSecrets.com and click the button that says 'Get Access'. Fill out your details and you'll be given instant access to the programme.

Imagine, you could be starting the programme today and be on your way to securing your Paula in the next few weeks. You too could be walking the #StagerBoss LIVE stage for your six-figure award in the next year. I can't wait to congratulate you.

Visit StagingBusinessSecrets.com to find out more.

Let's get to work.

You've made it – congratulations! You have the first steps in your hand; now go and take action. Don't let anything stop you. You want more; now go out and claim it.

Hopefully, I'll meet you again, whether that be in the near future or in Staging Business Secrets, should you choose to go all in and invest in your success. Meanwhile, I wish you the best of luck. This is your time to shine. I look forward to hearing your story.

Your Action List

As promised, here is your action list for the entire book. This acts as your home-staging launch guide. My best advice is to read each chapter again and implement the recommended list immediately after reading. You'll be launching your business in no time.

Chapter 3 'Choose Your Fuel Source' action list:

Answer these questions:

- Is pain driving you currently?

- Can you use this as a fuel source to drive you to your vision?

- How can you tap into purpose as a fuel source?

Chapter 4 'Design Your Vision And Map Out Your Goals' action list:

- Following the method outlined in this chapter, create your vision board for your life and business.

- Write down your income BHAG.

- Draw the stair diagram from this chapter and add your BHAG to the top step.

- Work out your monthly survival budget and add it to your diagram.

- Put your monthly survival budget everywhere to ensure it's always on your mind.

Chapter 5 'Reverse Engineer Your Dream Income' action list:

- Work out your yearly survival budget.

- Decide where you would like to position yourself in the market.

- Choose your example average price.

- Use the 8 Installation Calculation.

- Write your statement: 'I need to stage X properties per year to earn my desired income'.

Chapter 6 'Choose Your Signature Service' action list:

- Choose your signature service.

Chapter 7 'Game-Changing Clients: Who Are They And How Do You Find Them?' action list:

- Create your dream client avatar.

- Write a list of your client's aspirations (their goals, dreams and desires).

- Write a list of your client's pain points.

- Create your client transformation statement.

Chapter 8 'Brand Your Business Like a Boss' action list:

- Decide on your brand name.

- Create your brand inspiration board.

- Create your own logo/brand-asset document or outsource.

- Implement your branding across your online platforms.

- Consider your offline branding (but don't let this stop you from launching).

Chapter 9 'Your Personal Brand Is What Sells' action list:

- Decide on your brand hooks:
  - Your A to B Transformation
  - Your challenges and obstacles
  - Your experience
  - Your achievements
- Write your brand story.
- Upload your brand story to your social-media platforms and website (if applicable).

Chapter 10 'Launch Your Brand With A Bang' action list:

- Ensure you have completed the launch list:
  - You've chosen your signature service (see Chapter 6).
  - You've created your beta brand – remember, don't spend too long on this.
  - You've set up your on-brand social-media profiles.
  - You have a contract in place for when a client wants to go ahead.

- Plan seven to ten days of online pre-launch build-up.

- Plan your offline launch:

  - Write a list of your connections.

  - Reach out to your list.

- Plan and implement launch day, including:

  - Video announcement (preferably live)

  - Social-media post

  - Brand-launch event

  - Connecting with local businesses

  - Creating a launch offer

- Plan your post-launch:

  - Follow up with meetings or calls.

  - Schedule your one-month-in-advance of content (see Chapter 12 for more on online content).

Chapter 11 'Get Your First Paula Offline' action list:

- Outline your local networking events:

  - The name of the event

  - Link to book

  - Date and location of the event

- Frequency (they are usually monthly)

- Audience size

- Name and details of the organiser

- Join the Facebook group for each event (if applicable).

- Connect with host of networking events / research exhibitions you could secure a speaking slot at.

- Consider hosting your own event (longer term).

- Write a list of potential partnerships (estate agents, rental agents, existing clients, sponsorship opportunities) and reach out.

Chapter 12 'Explode Your Brand On Social' action list:

- Write a statement of committing – how will you show up every day?

- Set up your profiles on Facebook, Instagram and LinkedIn.

- Brainstorm five ideas for 'You' and 'Objection' content.

- Write ten captions in total and schedule these on social media.

The Author

Not many people can say they've started two success-ful businesses from scratch, built a £1m brand in their teens, travelled the world speaking, including on the TEDx stage, won fourteen national and international business and entrepreneur awards, been invited to din-ner with the Prime Minister and become a best-selling author with an endorse-ment from Netflix. And even fewer people can say they've done all that – and so much more – before they were twenty-four years old.

CEO and founder of ThePropertyStagers and the UK Young Entrepreneur of the Year 2020, Liv Conlon is tenacious and entrepreneurial to her core. She left school aged sixteen and beat the odds, turning her vision into a profitable reality and founding her first business, ThePropertyStagers. At nineteen, she built a £1m brand in an industry that was in its infancy, so Liv knows a thing or two about building an internationally recognisable, scalable business and personal brand. Liv now uses her own success and experience to help entrepreneurs go from best-kept secret to industry-leading authority.

Connect with Liv via:

f www.facebook.com/olivia.conlon.5

◎ www.instagram.com/oliviaconlon

Printed in Great Britain
by Amazon

21040412R00132